BOSTON
RED SOX
TRIVIA TEASERS

RICHARD PENNINGTON

TRAILS BOOKS
Madison, Wisconsin

Library of Congress Control Number: 2007923663
ISBN 13: 978-1-931599-82-5
ISBN 10: 1-931599-82-3

Editor: Mark Knickelbine
Designer: Colin Harrington
Photos: National Baseball Hall of Fame Library
Cooperstown, NY

Printed in the United States of America.
12 11 10 09 08 07   6 5 4 3 2 1

Trails Books, a division of Big Earth Publishing
923 Williamson Street • Madison, WI 53703
(800) 258-5830 • www.trailsbooks.com

Table of CONTENTS

Cy Young, the winner of 511 games, played with Boston from 1901 to 1908.

Chapter One
THE AMERICANS

So much are the Red Sox associated with the city of Boston, it is hard to imagine that they were not always the Red Sox. Nor were they the first team in town—far from it. The National League was well-established by the time the new team arrived, and one of the league's top clubs had deep roots in Boston. The Boston Red Stockings had begun play in 1876, although their name was soon changed to the Beaneaters. They were later known as the Doves, the Rustlers, the Braves, the Bees, and the Braves again (for simplicity's sake, let's just call them the Braves). But the club's owners could not have been pleased to hear that the fledgling American League planned to put a team in Boston.

The new team did not even have a name other than its official one: the Boston American League Baseball Company. Only in 1908 did owner John I. Taylor decide to call them the Red Sox. As if to emphasize his choice, he ordered new uniforms featuring bright red hosiery. Even so, sportswriters in the first seven years were shameless about giving names of their own, such as the Americans, the Pilgrims, the Puritans, or the Plymouth Rocks. But Americans was used most often, much as their intracity rivals were sometimes referred to as the Boston Nationals.

The Braves were decimated when many of their top players signed with the new team. Only once in the first 13 years of the twentieth century did they have a winning season, and soon they were supplanted in the hearts of local baseball fans by the Americans. The Braves had no intention of sharing South End Grounds with these interlopers. Thus Huntington Avenue Grounds came into existence. It served as the home of the Americans/Red Sox from 1901 to 1911.

Q What occupied the site of Huntington Avenue Grounds prior to the ballpark?

A Located in a poor Irish neighborhood of Boston, it had previously been the site of a circus. Only a railroad track separated it from South End Grounds. Warehouses, factories, breweries, and stables surrounded the park, which consisted of three cement grandstands, rickety wooden bleachers, and a covered segment along the third base line. Abnormal facilities were the norm back then, so nobody thought much of center field sloping uphill (the fence was a whopping 635 feet from home plate), the knee-high weeds, the patches of sand where grass refused to grow, or the outfield toolshed that was in play. Huntington Avenue Grounds, which seated 11,500 fans, was razed after Fenway Park was built in 1912.

Q What was the cost of building Huntington Avenue Grounds?

A $35,000.

Q The Red Sox were at Huntington Avenue Grounds for 11 seasons. How did they do in that time?

A They compiled an 850-781 record, won one World Series title, and had eight managers and three owners.

Q What were the dimensions of Huntington Avenue Grounds?

A When it opened, they were 350 feet to left field, 530 to center, and 280 to right. In its last season as home of the Sox, it had changed slightly—350 feet to left, 635 to center, and 320 to right.

Q How was attendance for the Americans in 1901?

A The team (which went 79-57) drew 289,448 fans or an average of 4,195 per game.

Q Who was the first owner of the Boston Americans?

A Charles Somers. This Cleveland businessman had made a fortune in coal, lumber, and shipping, and was one of the three founders (along with Ban Johnson and Charles Comiskey) of the American League. Somers also owned the Cleveland Indians from 1910 to 1915. A lavish spender in the early years, financial difficulties eventually drove him from the game.

Q Who were the members of that first AL team in Boston?

A First basemen Buck Freeman and Larry McLean; shortstop Fred Parent; pitchers George Winter, Fred Mitchell, Cy Young, and Ted Lewis; outfielders Tommy Dowd, Charles "Chick" Stahl, and Charlie Hemphill; second baseman Hobe Ferris; catchers Ossee Schreckengost and Lou Criger; and manager and third baseman Jimmy Collins.

Q How did it go on opening day in 1903?

A Some 8,376 fans saw Boston defeat the Philadelphia A's, 9-4, in the morning game of a Patriot's Day doubleheader. A much bigger crowd of 27,658 was there for the second game when Connie Mack's Athletics won, 10-7; that game featured two future Hall of Fame hurlers, Eddie Plank and Cy Young.

Q Since 1895, he had been a standout at the plate and as a third baseman with the Braves. So when he jumped to the city's fledgling American League franchise in 1901, he brought the team instant credibility. Who was he?

A Jimmy Collins. His defense at the hot spot would be the gold standard for half a century. As player and manager, he led the team to the 1903 World Series title and an American League pennant in '04. Collins ended his career in 1908 with the Philadelphia A's.

Q What landmark games were played at Huntington Avenue Grounds?

A Boston won the American League pennant in 1903 and hosted the Pittsburgh Pirates in the first four World Series games ever played, winning the Series, 5-3. And Cy Young pitched the first perfect game of the twentieth century there on May 5, 1904.

Q What was the attendance at Huntington Avenue Grounds for Game 1 of the first World Series?

A 16,242.

Q Was there a crowd-control issue in Boston during the 1903 World Series?

A Yes. So many fans spilled over onto the field that police used rubber hoses and bats to move them back enough for the games to be played. The fans remained in the outfield, just 250 feet from home plate.

Q What Broadway tune gained notoriety when it was adopted by Boston fans in the '03 Series?

A "Tessie."

Q What were the lyrics to the chorus?

A "Tessie, you make me feel so badly / Why don't you turn around? / Tessie, you know I love you madly / Babe, my heart weighs about a pound / Don't blame me if I ever doubt you / You know I wouldn't live without you / Tessie, you are the only, only, only." They were sometimes altered derisively, such as this line directed toward Pirates star Honus Wagner: "Honus, why do you hit so badly?"

Q What Boston-area punk band revived the song in 2004?

A The Dropkick Murphys; backup vocals were done by Johnny Damon, Bronson Arroyo, and other Sox players.

Q This man owned a tavern in Boston's South End where a loyal cadre of fans (who called themselves "the Royal Rooters") gathered to drink and cheer the team. Who was he?

A Michael T. "Nuf Ced" McGreevey. His saloon, Third Base, was located at 940 Columbus Avenue. Booze, baseball, and betting were always in season there.

Q Young's real name is Denton True. How did he come by his nickname?

A "Cy" was the shortened form of "Cyclone." Young, a native of rural Ohio, claimed that barns and fences were damaged by the speed of his blindingly fast pitches.

Q How was Young honored in August 1908?

A A special day was set aside to recognize his longevity and greatness. All American League action was halted, and a group of all-stars came to Boston to face Young and the Red Sox.

Q Lou Criger is a forgotten name from long ago. Who was he?

A His career spanned 1896 to 1912, and he spent exactly half of that time in Boston. Criger was a small, agile, and light-hitting (.221 batting average) player. Most of all, though, he was Cy Young's favorite catcher—for three different franchises.

Q Criger was also a man of integrity, was he not?

A Evidently. Some gamblers offered him a bribe to throw the 1903 Series, but he refused, catching every inning of every game for the victorious Americans.

Q How did right fielder Buck Freeman do in the 1903 season?

A Quite well. His heavy hitting had a lot to do with the team winning the title. Freeman paced the AL with 13 homers and 104 RBI.

Q What were the highlights of Freeman's career?

A He was an erratic fielder but one of the top hitters of the dead-ball era, as can be seen in the 25 home runs he hit for Washington in 1899. Freeman played 535 straight games for Boston, a record not broken until Everett Scott came along 15 years later.

Q What 150-pound pitcher won 43 games for Boston in 1904 and 1905?

A Jesse Tannehhill.

Q With 25,000 fans looking on, he threw a wild pitch in the ninth inning of the final game of the 1904 season, allowing the Americans to win the AL pennant. Who was he?

A "Happy Jack" Chesbro of the New York Highlanders (soon renamed the Yankees). He started 51 games that year and finished 48 of them.

Q Why was there no World Series in 1904?

A The inaugural version in '03 had been a resounding success, but some NL owners were still not convinced that the junior league was up to their standards. It was canceled primarily because John Brush, owner of the NL champion New York Giants, would not compromise.

Q And did Brush ever come around?

A Yes. He soon regretted his decision and even proposed what would be known as "the Brush Rules," by which the World Series have been held ever since. Most important was the creation of a commission overseeing both leagues and the sport itself.

Q What is the longest losing streak in team history?

A The 1906 Americans lost 20 in a row.

Q Recall the sad story of Charles "Chick" Stahl.

A He was an excellent outfielder with the Boston Braves from 1897 to 1900 and with the Americans for six more seasons. He had three triples in the Americans' 1903 World Series victory over heavily favored Pittsburgh. Manager of the team in 1906, Stahl was beset by pressures on and off the field. After 1907 spring training, the team was at a resort in West Baden, Indiana, when he committed suicide by drinking four ounces of carbolic acid. He left a note that read, "Boys, I just couldn't help it. You drove me to it." The truth is, he had been blackmailed by a woman who bore his child out of wedlock.

Q Spring training 100 years ago was rather different from today. What did the team do back then?

A Owner John I. Taylor sent them to Hot Springs, Arkansas. To get in shape, the players would take long hikes (in full uniform, including spiked shoes) in the Ozarks.

Q Who was Cy Young's successor in Boston?

A "Smoky" Joe Wood, who was purchased from a minor league team in Kansas City in 1908. Three years later, he won 23 games, threw a no-hitter, and struck out 15 batters in one game—a record that would stand until 1961. Wood had his greatest season in 1912, going 34-5 and winning three games in the World Series (in which Boston beat the New York Giants). The nickname derived from his fastball; both Walter Johnson and Satchel Paige said that no one could throw harder than Wood. A hand injury in 1913 ended his brilliant pitching career but he moved to the outfield and kept playing with the Sox and Indians through 1922. He later spent 20 years as the baseball coach at Yale.

Q He won 65 games for the Americans between 1902 and 1904, and threw a no-hitter in '05. Who was this fine pitcher?

A Bill Dinneen, who later served as an umpire for almost 30 years.

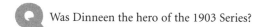

Q Was Dinneen the hero of the 1903 Series?

A You could say that. He won three games in four tries and had a 2.06 ERA.

Q Taylor had bought the team from Henry Killilea in 1904 and sold it to James McAleer eight years later—but with the proviso that he (Taylor) owned the new park and would derive rents therefrom in years to follow. And who was McAleer?

A He had forged a 14-year career with the NL's Cleveland Spiders and the AL's Cleveland Blues and St. Louis Browns from 1889 to 1907. McAleer managed the Blues, Browns, and Senators for 11 seasons before buying the Red Sox .

Q Why did McAleer sell the Sox?

A He sold them because of a long-running feud with American League president Ban Johnson.

Q How many games did Cy Young complete and win in his long career?

A 749 and 511, respectively; these are records that will probably never be broken in the modern era.

Q This New England native played third base for the Sox, A's, and Indians from 1908 to 1924. Who was he?

A Larry Gardner, who drove in the winning run in the final game of the 1912 World Series against the Giants with a 10th-inning sacrifice fly. He later became baseball coach and athletic director at the University of Vermont.

Q He must have been the worst shortstop in the major leagues, given that he averaged 51 errors per year from 1908 to 1913. Who was this man with the stone hands?

A Heinie Wagner, who also managed the Sox in 1930 to a league's worst record of 52-102.

Q Outfielder Harry Hooper holds what distinction?

A He played on four championship teams for Boston—1912, 1915, 1916, and 1918.

Q Identify the person who uttered these words: "I like the sound of base hits better than grand opera, if my team is making them."

A Cy Young.

Q The 1909 Sox drew 8,920 fans per game. When would that record be topped?

A Not until 1940, when the average was 9,066.

Q What did Detroit Tigers star Ty Cobb do to the Sox on August 18, 1911?

A He stole home in the first inning of the Tigers' 9-4 victory.

Q What was the last game played at Huntington Avenue Grounds?

A On October 7, 1911, the Red Sox beat the Washington Senators, 8-1.

Q What firm was engaged to design Fenway Park?

A Osborn Engineering was given the task of fitting the park into the asymmetrical plot of land Taylor had purchased for $300,000. Osborn was also told to retain the orientation of Huntington Avenue Grounds, in which the third-base line pointed nearly due north. McLaughlin Construction Company built it. Both, by the way, were retained when the park was rebuilt in 1934.

Q What streets bordered Fenway when it was built in 1912?

A Brooklyn Avenue, Lansdowne Street, Ipswich Street, Van Ness Street, and Jersey Street.

Q When was groundbreaking?

A Ground was broken on September 25, 1911, and Fenway Park opened on April 20 of the following year (the same day Tiger Stadium [then called Navin Field] opened in Detroit). The total cost of construction was $650,000, and the original seating capacity was 26,000.

Q What event five days earlier kept the unveiling of Fenway Park off the front pages of newspapers in the Hub City?

A The sinking of the *Titanic*.

Q Where did the stadium come by its name?

A A number of "fens" or marshes were to be found in the Back Bay area of Boston, where owner John Taylor chose to build. It should be noted that Taylor owned Fenway Realty—perhaps an early naming-rights decision.

Q What was the first game ever held at Fenway Park?

A On April 9, 1912, the Red Sox beat Harvard University in an exhibition game played in a snowstorm.

Q And the first major league game?

A The home opener was delayed for a week due to rains, which caused most of the pomp and ceremony to be scrapped. The first pitch was thrown from the stands by Boston mayor John "Honey Fitz" Fitzgerald, grandfather of future president John F. Kennedy. (Fitzgerald had a notion to own the team, but AL president Ban Johnson disallowed it.) As to the first game, Boston beat New York, 7-6.

Q He, along with Duffy Lewis and Harry Hooper, formed Boston's "million-dollar outfield" in the early 1910s. He played for 22 years (9 with the Red Sox, 11 with the Indians, and 1 each with the Senators and A's). Name him.

A Tris Speaker. Swift of foot (he had 433 stolen bases), outstanding defensively, and a master with the bat (.345 career average), he could do it all. It's true he only hit 117 home runs, but it was the "dead-ball era," the period before the introduction of the cork-centered ball when home runs were a relative rarity. Ty Cobb considered Speaker the finest player he ever competed against. He also managed the Indians from 1919 to 1926 and was elected to the Hall of Fame in only its second year of existence.

Q Speaker was named 1912 American League MVP. What other Boston players have won the award?

A Jimmie Foxx (1938), Ted Williams (1946 and 1949), Jackie Jensen (1958), Carl Yastrzemski (1967), Jim Rice (1978), Mo Vaughan (1995), and Roger Clemens (1986).

Q How did the Sox win their second World Series title?

A It was a 4-3-1 defeat of the New York Giants, featuring some great pitching by Smoky Joe Wood and Christy Mathewson. Errors in the 10th inning of the final game by center fielder Fred Snodgrass and first baseman Fred Merkle let Boston come back from a 2-1 deficit to win, 3-2. Oddly enough, the stands were less than half full when they won the 1912 championship.

Q How did Tris Speaker do in 1912?

A He hit .383 with 53 doubles, had eight inside-the-park home runs, and led the Red Sox to a World Series title.

Q He was a graduate of the University of Illinois and played nine years with Boston, Washington, and the New York Highlanders. Unsuccessful as a player-manager in two seasons with the Senators, he did much better with the Sox in 1912. Who was he?

A Jake Stahl (no relation to Chick), whose team won the 1912 World Series against John McGraw's Giants. But a falling-out with his players led to Stahl's resignation midway through the 1913 season.

Q After Stahl quit, who took his place as manager?

A Bill Carrigan, who had been with the franchise since 1906 as a part-time catcher. As a player-manager, he led the Sox to a second-place finish in 1914 and then won it all the next two seasons. Then, at the very peak of his profession, Carrigan quit and went home to Lewiston, Maine, to become a banker. He managed the Sox again from 1927 to 1929, but with vastly different results—last place all three years.

Q What was Carrigan's nickname?

A "Rough," and he surely was as a player and manager. In the often-brutal dead-ball era, he helped set the tone. Carrigan had the grudging respect of opponents such as Ty Cobb and his own teammates, once taking care of Tris Speaker (no softie, himself) in a clubhouse fistfight.

Q Carrigan did one more very significant thing for the Sox. What was it?

A He nurtured a young Babe Ruth.

Q The Red Sox of the early 1910s were divided by religious affiliation. Detail that matter.

A It was the Catholics (dubbed the "KCs" for Knights of Columbus), led by George "Duffy" Lewis, Carrigan, John O'Brien, and Harry Hooper, versus the Protestants (the "Masons"), led by Tris Speaker and Joe Wood.

Q A rookie in 1914, this shortstop weighed just 148 pounds, so he didn't have much pop at the plate. But he was quite an iron man, both with Boston and then the New York Yankees. Who was he?

A Everett Scott.

Q This man was equipped with an engineering degree before he began his major league career and even offered a few tips during the construction of Fenway Park. Who was he?

A Harry Hooper. He was the first player to hit a home run to lead off both games of a doubleheader (a mark later matched by Rickey Henderson). His last five years were spent with the White Sox.

Q This fine catcher already had a World Series title (with the Philadelphia A's) to his credit before joining the Red Sox in 1918. Who was he?

A Wally Schang.

Q What else do we remember Schang for?

A A 20-game hitting streak in 1916, throwing out six would-be base-stealers in one game, hitting a home run from both sides of the plate in one game, ranking seventh among catchers in stolen bases (121), and being the only player in major league history to win a Series with three different clubs—the A's, Red Sox, and Yankees.

Q This knuckleball specialist was 41-48 for Boston before being traded to the White Sox in 1912. In time, he became one of the premier pitchers in the AL, winning more than 20 games thrice. Who was he? Hint: He was involved in the most infamous scandal in baseball history.

A Eddie Cicotte, and we are talking about the Black Sox scandal of 1919. His $6,000 contract included a provision for a $10,000 bonus if he won 30 games. He had 29 with time to spare, but abstemious owner Charles Comiskey ordered manager Kid Gleason to bench him. Cicotte, who won one game and lost two against the Reds in that Series, confessed to helping throw the Series and then recanted. Nonetheless, he and seven others were banned from the game by commissioner Kennesaw Mountain Landis.

Q Who was Hubert "Dutch" Leonard?

A Not to be confused with Emil "Dutch" Leonard, who pitched for the Dodgers, Senators, Phillies, and Cubs from 1933 to 1953, Hubert had an 11-year career with the Red Sox and Tigers a generation before Emil. He compiled a 1.01 ERA in 1914 and won one game each for the Sox' World Series champions of 1915 and 1916.

Q When Ban Johnson engineered McAleer's removal as owner of the Red Sox in 1914, who purchased the team?

A Joseph L. Lannin, a French-Canadian who had immigrated to Boston as a poor teenager and whose life became a Horatio Alger story when he gained success as a real estate magnate. Previously a minority owner of the Boston Braves, he bought the Sox as well as the rights to a promising young pitcher named Babe Ruth.

Q How did that happen?

A The Baltimore Orioles of the International League were trying to stay afloat, so their owner, Jack Dunn, was selling his best players. During a road trip to Washington, Lannin rode the train to Baltimore and made a deal with Dunn: Ruth, pitcher Ernie Shore, and catcher Ben Egan for somewhere between $20,000 and $25,000. Ruth was a good prospect but a prospect nonetheless. It was not an especially significant player transaction at the time.

Q Was Ruth in such demand?

A No. Dunn had offered him to Connie Mack of the Philadelphia A's and was turned down flat.

Q Ruth arrived in Boston on the morning of July 11, 1914, and was the starting pitcher for that day's game against Cleveland. How did he do?

A He held the Indians to five hits in six innings with one strikeout, but three hits and a sacrifice in the seventh tied the game and he was taken out for reliever Dutch Leonard.

Q Two games in the 1914 World Series were played at Fenway Park, but the Red Sox were not participants. What was the story?

A Boston's "Miracle" Braves, in last place on July 19, won 51 of their last 67 games on the way to a surprise title. Their own park, South End Grounds (first used in 1894), was hopelessly outdated so the Red Sox proved to be good neighbors, leasing Fenway for the last six weeks of the regular season and then the Series, in which George Stallings's team swept the A's.

Q How did the Braves return the favor to their American League brothers?

A Braves Field, which had a seating capacity of 40,000, was used by the Sox for their "home" games during the 1915 and 1916 World Series triumphs.

Who made this observation of Ruth's career? "Sometimes I still can't believe what I saw. This 19-year-old kid, crude, poorly educated, only lightly brushed by the social veneer we call civilization, gradually transformed into the idol of American youth and the symbol of baseball the world over—a man loved by more people and with an intensity of feeling that perhaps has never been equaled before or since. I saw a man transformed into something pretty close to a god."

 Harry Hooper, a Red Sox teammate in the late 1910s.

 What was Ruth's last hurrah?

He was playing with the Boston Braves on May 25, 1935, when he hit three homers in Pittsburgh. One week later, batting just .181, he announced he was quitting at the same time the Braves said he was released. Ruth held 56 major league records at the time.

What transpired on September 16, 1915, at Fenway Park?

Red Sox rookie reliever Carl Mays hit Detroit's Ty Cobb on the wrist, prompting Cobb to fling his bat at Mays. The crowd erupted and threw bottles at Cobb. At game's end, he needed a police escort to leave the field. The Tigers won, 6-1.

Q Game 2 of the 1915 World Series took place at the cozy Baker Bowl in Philadelphia. What notable person attended?

A President Woodrow Wilson, in the company of his baseball-loving fiancée, Edith Galt. The Phillies, who took Game 1, lost the next four. The Sox' pitching was so dominant that Babe Ruth did not make a mound appearance, and he only came to bat once as a pinch-hitter. The winner of the final game was George "Rube" Foster.

Q When the team returned home from Philly, there was a big celebration, right?

A Wrong. Some fans had prepared to gather at the train station, but the team arrived early and dispersed. Anyway, Carrigan had made it clear that he expected to win the championship.

Q This man stood just 5' 7", but he could really pitch. He no-hit the Yankees on June 21, 1916, (the first no-no ever thrown at Fenway Park) and helped the Sox win World Series titles back to back. Identify him.

A Rube Foster. Despite his 58-34 record over five seasons, Boston traded him to Cincinnati after the 1917 season. Rather than play with the Reds, Foster quit baseball.

Q He played outfield for the 1916 World Series champs but didn't really hit his stride until he joined the Athletics and became one of the first true power hitters, smacking 77 homers in a three-year span. Who was he?

A Clarence "Tilly" Walker. His .549 slugging percentage in 1922 is particularly impressive.

Q What was unusual about Walker's home run against the Yankees at Fenway Park on June 20, 1916?

A It was the Sox' only home run at home that season.

Q What was the date of a classic pitching duel in which Babe Ruth of the Red Sox beat Walter Johnson of the Washington Senators, 1-0, in 13 innings at Fenway Park?

A August 15, 1916.

Tris Speaker had moved on to Cleveland by 1916, but the Red Sox repeated as champs of the baseball world. What happened in that Series?

Their opponents were the Brooklyn Robins (renamed the Dodgers in 1931), whose outfielder, Casey Stengel, batted .364. But they could only manage one win against Boston. Game 2 featured Ruth pitching 14 innings; when the game was won in dramatic fashion in the 14th, he grabbed manager Bill Carrigan in a bear hug and shouted, "I told you I could take care of those National League sons of bitches!"

On April 24, 1917, the Sox were subjected to a no-hitter at Fenway Park. Who did the dirty deed?

George Mogridge of the Yankees.

This graduate of Guilford College was one of the mainstays on the Red Sox' pitching staff when they won the 1915 and 1916 World Series. Who was he?

Ernie Shore. In the former season, he was 19-8 and had an ERA of 1.64.

Q What was Shore's most famous moment?

A It came on June 13, 1917, against the Senators at Fenway. His team-mate, Babe Ruth, had just walked the first batter when he got into a spirited disagreement with the umpire and gave him a little love tap before being ejected. On came Shore in relief. The man on first tried to steal and was thrown out, and Shore then retired the next 26 batters. The Red Sox won, 4-0, and Shore had a weird no-hitter.

Q In the 1918 season, abbreviated some 30 games by World War I, Boston won the AL pennant by two-and-a-half games over Cleveland. How did the Sox do in their third World Series in four years?

A They beat the Chicago Cubs, four games to two. Boston's home games were back at Fenway, but the Cubs chose to use Comiskey Park, the bigger facility of their cross-town rivals, the White Sox. The Series was marred by rumors of a fix (as had happened in previous Series) and the threat of a players' strike over the issue of low gate receipts. Ruth, who won Games 1 and 4, ran his streak of scoreless innings to 29 $\frac{2}{3}$. Who could have known that 86 years would pass before the Red Sox won another World Series?

Q What did a bleacher seat at Fenway Park cost for a regular season game in 1918?

A 25 cents.

Q Identify the surprise hero of the 1918 World Series.

A George Whiteman. What an unusual career—he had played three games with the Sox back in 1907, roamed the minor leagues for six years, had 11 games with New York in 1913, returned to the minors, and then was back with Boston for 71 games in 1918. Whiteman delivered several key hits and made some big catches in the outfield during that Series. He never played in another big league game.

Q Who was Harry Frazee?

A A native of Peoria, Illinois, he had become successful with light theatrical productions, then branched into real estate. Whatever Frazee did, it seemingly turned to money. He had sought to buy a major league baseball team since 1909 and finally succeeded after the 1916 season. For $675,000 (half on credit, however), he purchased the Red Sox from Lannin and Fenway Park from the Taylor family. Frazee, an outsider to Boston and the baseball world as a whole, was the subject of much speculation—such as that he might raze the park, sell that valuable land, and move to the far more spacious Braves Field to reap a big profit.

Q Was there ever a chance that the New York Yankees would move to Boston?

A As a matter of fact, yes. Boston owner Harry Frazee was having legal and financial problems. One of many discussions held between Frazee and the Yankees' owners (and AL president Ban Johnson) was the possibility of moving the New York franchise to New England, merging with or even supplanting the Red Sox.

Q Carl Mays, who won two games in the 1918 World Series, was surly and unpopular with fans, opponents, and teammates alike. In July 1919, in a game against the White Sox, Mays quit the mound because he doubted the defensive efforts of his teammates. What resulted?

A In defiance of AL president Ban Johnson, Red Sox owner Harry Frazee traded him to the Yankees. While with New York, Mays threw the pitch that struck Cleveland batter Ray Chapman in the skull, causing his death. Mays would also become the first pitcher ever to win 20 games for three different teams—Red Sox, Yanks, and Reds.

Q How did Ruth do in 1919?

A His team, the defending champs, finished 20 ½ games out of first place, but the big man (he had become rather rotund by that time) had a splendid year: a record 29 home runs, .322 batting average, and 114 RBI, and he still pitched in 17 games. Nevertheless, Barrow, Frazee, and some Boston sports scribes were convinced it was an aberration and that Ruth had hit his peak.

Q Frazee's various problems led him to do what?

A Trade or sell some very good players—including pitchers Waite Hoyt, Carl Mays, and Herb Pennock, catcher Wally Schang, shortstop Everett Scott, third baseman Joe Dugan, and, of course, Babe Ruth—to the Yanks. No fewer than 11 ex-Sox players were on the 1923 New York team that won the World Series.

Q The 1919 Red Sox finished far behind the White Sox, and there were endless struggles among Ruth, Barrow, and Frazee. How was attendance at home games that year?

A A total of just over 417,000—far less than followed the championship seasons of 1912, 1915, and 1916.

The Red Sox beat the Philadelphia Phillies, four games to one, in the 1915 World Series. Babe Ruth (back row, sixth from left) was in his second year with Boston and still a full-time pitcher.

Chapter Two
BABE MOVES ON

How Babe Ruth came to be sent to the New York Yankees is a rather complicated matter, full of myths and untruths. First of all, Harry Frazee did not sell Ruth to finance his Broadway production of *No, No, Nanette* (the show was not staged until five years later). In fact, Frazee and AL president Ban Johnson had been butting heads for a while, and the issue came to a boil in the summer of 1919. The ever-erratic Ruth had jumped the team before the final game of the season and was constantly demanding more money. The owner was fed up with Ruth's hijinks and determined to trade or sell him. But due to a split of the American League into factions (New York, Boston, and Chicago, on one side, were known as the "insurrectos," and the other clubs were the "loyal five"), his options were limited. The White Sox offered Shoeless Joe Jackson—remember, this was just before the Black Sox scandal—plus $60,000. But the Yankees' owners made an all-cash offer of $125,000 and a $350,000 loan against the mortgage on Fenway Park. The Bambino became property of the Yankees on January 3, 1920.

In an interview with the press two days later, Frazee said: "It would be impossible to start next season with Ruth and have a smooth-working machine. Ruth had become simply impossible, and the Boston club could no longer put up with his eccentricities. I think the Yankees are taking a gamble. While Ruth is undoubtedly the greatest hitter the game has ever seen, he is likewise one of the most selfish and inconsiderate men ever to have put on a baseball uniform."

Be that as it may, Ruth proceeded to become the focal point of the greatest dynasty in pro sports history, racking up staggering statistics, and his fame drove the popularity of baseball throughout the United States and worldwide. The team Ruth left, the Red Sox, almost immediately became one of the worst in all of the major leagues. It is only a slight stretch to say that Sox fans had little to smile about for two decades—until the arrival of Ted Williams.

Q Everybody knows that in 1995, Cal Ripken of the Orioles broke Lou Gehrig's record for most consecutive games played. But who held the record before Gehrig?

A Everett "the Deacon" Scott, a shortstop who had a 12-year career with the Red Sox, Yankees, Senators, White Sox, and Reds. He appeared in 1,307 straight games from June 20, 1916 to May 6, 1925. Scott was a member of three World Series–winning teams with Boston and one with New York. He also led AL shortstops in fielding percentage for eight seasons in a row.

Q This pitcher, known as "the Knight of Kennett Square," was with the Red Sox from 1916 to 1922, but he really won his fame after a trade to the Yankees. Name him.

A Herb Pennock.

Q What Boston pitchers have hit grand slam home runs?

A Babe Ruth (1919), Lefty Grove (1935), Wes Ferrell (1936), and Ellis Kinder (1950).

Q When did Frazee sell the Sox?

A The team's performance plummeted in the early 1920s and Frazee, widely regarded as having given away a king's ransom to the Yankees in the form of Mays, Ruth, Scott, and others, sold the franchise to Robert Quinn, a crony of Ban Johnson. The price? $1.2 million.

Q What do we remember about Quinn?

A He had been GM of the St. Louis Browns for six seasons before purchasing the Sox. As owner and president, he strove to restore the credibility of the franchise, but Boston never got above sixth place in Quinn's 11 years at the helm. He later helped run the Brooklyn Dodgers and Boston Braves.

Q Quinn was quite a progenitor of baseball executives, wasn't he?

A He was. His son, John, would serve as GM of the Braves and Phillies; his grandson, Robert, would be GM of the Yankees, Reds, and Giants; and his great-grandson, Bob, is now the chief financial officer of the Brewers.

Q Who was the Red Sox' manager when they won the World Series title in 1918?

A Ed Barrow.

Q What was Barrow's baseball background?

A He had managed Toronto of the International League, as well as the Detroit Tigers, before coming to Boston. Barrow sometimes took credit for having turned Babe Ruth from a pitcher into a hitter, but the truth is he wanted to keep Ruth on the mound and only relented when it was an obvious thing to do. Barrow became GM of the Yankees in 1921 and proceeded to turn them into a juggernaut.

Q Name the manager of the Red Sox in 1921 and 1922.

A Hugh Duffy. In 1894, while with the Braves, he had batted .438—still the all-time record. Duffy had also managed the Phillies and White Sox, although without much distinction.

Q What else did Duffy do with the Sox?

A He was something of a coach emeritus in the late 1930s and into the 1940s, hired specifically to tutor Ted Williams.

Q What pitcher won 23 games for the 1921 Red Sox before being dealt to the Yankees?

A "Sad" Sam Jones.

Q Who was Jack Quinn?

A He was one of the last of the legal spitballers, due to a "grandfather clause." Quinn's career began in 1909 and did not conclude until 1933, during which time he won 247 games. Thirty-eight of them came with the Sox in the early 1920s.

Q This 5' 6" infielder played for the Tigers, Red Sox, Cubs, and Cards in the 1920s. He later managed the Browns, Pirates, and Braves (winning the 1957 World Series) before serving as GM of the expansion Los Angeles Angels. Who was he?

A Fred Haney.

Q What happened in Cleveland on July 7, 1923?

A The Sox were crushed by the Indians, 27-3. Curt Fullerton was the losing pitcher.

Q Howard Ehmke had quite a year in 1923. What was the story?

A After being traded from Detroit to Boston, he was the Red Sox' starting pitcher when Yankee Stadium opened on April 18, before a crowd of 74,217. (He gave up a home run to Babe Ruth and was the losing pitcher.) On May 18, Ehmke beat his former Tigers teammates and got into a rhubarb with Ty Cobb. On September 7, he threw a no-hitter against Philadelphia, thanks to an Athletics baserunning gaffe and a dubious call by one of the umps. Just four days later, back at Yankee Stadium, Ehmke gave up a single to the leadoff batter before retiring the next 27.

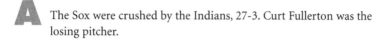

Q He came over from Detroit early in the 1923 season and was one of Boston's few bright spots for the rest of that decade. Who was he?

A Ira "Pete" Flagstead, who batted .294 for Boston and was a very good center fielder.

Q As a pitcher, he spent just one season (1923) in Boston, and it was utterly forgettable—winning one game, losing another, and earning a 5.43 ERA. During his four years out of the major leagues, this man reinvented himself, becoming one of the best hitters of his era. Who was he?

A Francis "Lefty" O'Doul, who compiled a .349 career batting average with the Giants, Phillies, and Dodgers, coached Joe DiMaggio and Ted Williams in the Pacific Coast League, and, beginning in 1931, was baseball's unofficial ambassador to Japan. O'Doul is largely responsible for the establishment of pro baseball in that country. Sadaharu Oh, Ichiro Suzuki, and others owe him a great debt.

Q Who managed the Sox for three years in the mid-1920s and won just 34 percent of his games?

A Lee Fohl, who had been only slightly more successful with the Indians and Browns before that.

Q Who was Red Ruffing?

A He pitched for the Red Sox from 1924 to 1929. A cursory look at his stats might indicate that he was terrible, but not so. In Ruffing's final two full seasons in Boston, he lost 47 games—mostly because he got so little offensive support. A trade to New York made Ruffing a totally different pitcher. He won 20 or more games four times for teams that won six World Series.

Q What happened at Fenway on May 8, 1926?

A The left-field bleachers burned down. And there was another blaze eight years later, as new owner Tom Yawkey was having the park refurbished.

Q What was new with the Red Sox in 1926?

A Some of their games were broadcast on radio; 22 years later, they were on television.

Q Who was the first visiting player to hit three home runs in one game at Fenway Park?

A Lou Gehrig of the Yankees, who did it on June 23, 1927.

Q Where have the Red Sox held spring training?

A Charlottesville, Virginia (1901), Augusta, Georgia (1902), Macon, Georgia (1903–1906), Little Rock, Arkansas (1907–1908), Hot Springs, Arkansas (1909–1910, 1912–1918, 1920–1923), Redondo Beach, California (1911), Tampa, Florida (1919), San Antonio, Texas (1924), New Orleans, Louisiana (1925–1927), Bradenton, Florida (1928–1929), Pensacola, Florida (1930–1931), Savannah, Georgia (1932), Sarasota, Florida (1933–1943, 1946–1958), Medford, Massachusetts (1943), Baltimore, Maryland (1944), Pleasantville, New Jersey (1945), Scottsdale, Arizona (1959–1965), Winter Haven, Florida (1966–1992), and Fort Myers, Florida (1993–present).

Q In the waning days of the 1928 season, American League bottom-dwellers Boston and Detroit met at Navin Field. The Tigers won, 8-0. How many fans were in attendance?

A Barely 400.

Q What light-hitting California native started at shortstop, third base, left field, center field, and right field on opening day from 1928 to 1932?

A Jack Rothrock.

Q What left fielder had a rookie-record 17 triples in 1929?

A Russ Scarritt.

Q The 1930 Red Sox were not much of a running team. Who led them in stolen bases?

A Tom Oliver and Bobby Reeves, both of whom had six.

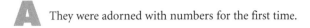

Q What was new with the Red Sox' uniforms in 1931?

A They were adorned with numbers for the first time.

Q Identify the slow-footed right fielder who set a major league record in 1931 by hitting 67 doubles.

A Earl Webb.

Q This big Tennessee native was traded from the Tigers to the Red Sox in the summer of 1932 and won the AL batting title (with a .367 average). Who was he?

A First baseman Dale Alexander.

Q Alexander suffered a knee injury the next year that ended his five-year career. What was the aftermath?

A He underwent an experimental treatment known as diathermy. It led to third-degree burns, gangrene, and the near loss of Alexander's leg.

Q How did the Sox do in '32?

A They were abysmal, with a 43-111 record, and drew just 182,150 fans to games at Fenway. That had to be one of the lowest points in the history of the franchise.

Q They called him "Deacon Danny." This quiet, bespectacled man was the Sox' best pitcher in the early 1930s, when New York gave up $50,000 and a couple of other players for him. Who was he?

A Danny MacFayden. He wasn't the pitching answer the Yankees had hoped for, so he was soon back in Boston—with the Braves, for whom he won 45 games from 1936 to 1938.

Q He spoke several languages, was widely viewed as the brainiest guy in the game, and his baseball card is said to be the only one on display at the headquarters of the CIA. Who was this unique individual?

A Moe Berg, who graduated from Princeton and, during his 15-year big league career with Brooklyn, the Chicago White Sox, Cleveland, Washington, and Boston, earned a law degree from Columbia and studied philosophy at the Sorbonne. In 1932 and 1934, he was part of two groups of players who toured Japan, teaching the game and serving as sports ambassadors. While in Tokyo, Berg addressed the legislature—in Japanese. He also surreptitiously took a 16mm camera to the tallest building in the city and made a panoramic film. After Pearl Harbor, its value grew immensely and was seen by Lt. Col. Jimmy Doolittle before his 1942 raid on Tokyo. Berg had a number of government-sponsored intelligence adventures during and after the war, in Central and South America, and all over Europe. Moe Berg, among the most charming, erudite, and mysterious players in the history of major league baseball, never wrote a memoir.

Q What was Duffy's Cliff?

A It was a 10-foot-high incline in front of the left field wall, lasting from the park's inception until 1933. Boston's star left fielder, Duffy Lewis, was adept at playing balls hit out there, and thus its name. When the Houston Astros opened their new Enron Field (since renamed Minute Maid Park) in 2000, it included an incline in center field—a tribute to Duffy's Cliff.

Q What job did Lewis later hold for 30 years?

A He was traveling secretary for the Boston/Milwaukee Braves.

Q Who purchased the Red Sox in 1933 and kept it in the family for the next 70 years?

A Tom Yawkey.

Q How did Yawkey come to own the team?

A His (very wealthy) adoptive father owned the Detroit Tigers from 1903 until his death in 1919, during which time young Yawkey came to love the game. His idol, Ty Cobb, urged him to buy a team if the opportunity ever arose. His $40 million inheritance became available on his 30th birthday—February 21, 1933—and four days later he had purchased the lowly Boston Red Sox from Bob Quinn and his associates for $1.5 million.

Q What were Yawkey's first steps?

A He hired Eddie Collins (whose 25-year career with the A's and White Sox [during which he came to bat nearly 10,000 times] had recently concluded) as GM, began paying his players fairly, put money into the Sox' farm system, and generally tried to instill a winning culture in a franchise that had lost it.

Q What was the scale of Yawkey's Fenway renovation?

A For roughly as much as he had paid for the franchise, Yawkey employed 750 skilled union workers who used 15,000 cubic yards of concrete, 550 tons of steel, and 500,000 feet of lumber. It resulted in a vastly bigger (seating capacity rose from 26,000 to 38,000) and better park.

Q Did Yawkey make money on his baseball investment?

A Not really. It is estimated that he lost more than $20 million during the years he owned the team. Yawkey died in 1976 and was inducted into the Hall of Fame four years later—still the only person to have made it in solely as an owner.

Q The Red Sox bought Lefty Grove from the A's in 1934 only to discover that he had a sore arm. Was the 1931 MVP washed up?

A He didn't do much that season but soon returned to form, winning 83 games over the next five years. Although Grove was good, he was not the dominant pitcher he had been with Philly.

Q Grove's record over 17 years was an impressive 300-141. But it could have been even more so. What's the story?

A He had been signed by a minor league owner who had no affiliation with the majors, so he kept Grove down on the farm for five years. During that time, he won more than 100 games before the A's bought his rights. Such was the reality of pro baseball players in those days.

Q What was Grove's record at Fenway Park?

A His record was 55-17, a winning percentage of .764.

Q What San Francisco native was a well-established star with the Senators before joining the BoSox in 1935?

A Joe Cronin. When Boston bought his contract, it got an excellent batter (but an average shortstop—he committed 510 errors in his 20-year career) and manager. Cronin continued to fulfill both roles for two seasons after his retirement as a player in 1945.

Q When Cronin was sold to the Sox, what did the cash-strapped Senators get for him?

A $250,000, a gargantuan amount in the Great Depression.

Q What did Cronin do after managing the Red Sox?

A He became GM for 11 years. During that time, he made a number of aggressive trades but the team was in a slow decline. Cronin also served as the American League president from 1959 to 1973.

Q How many Red Sox games did Cronin manage?

A 2,007—of which 1,071 were victories and 916 were defeats.

Q Besides the 1934 renovation/expansion, what other major changes have occurred at the friendly confines of Fenway Park?

A The bullpens were moved from fair territory to right field in 1940. Upper-deck seats were installed in 1946, and lights were added in 1947. A message board was installed above the center field bleachers in 1976. Private suites were added to the roof in 1983, and a glassed-in seating section was built behind home plate in 1988. Auxiliary press boxes were added in 1999. And in 2003, nearly 300 coveted seats were placed atop the Green Monster.

Q What is the Green Monster?

A It is a very famous wall that graces left field at Fenway Park. Replacing a 25-foot wall that had existed there before, it was built in 1934 and is 37 feet high, 240 feet long, and built of 15 tons of iron. It was not until 1947, when advertisements for such items as beer, razor blades, soap, and vitamins were covered with green paint, that it got its moniker. A manual scoreboard was operated there until 1975.

Q What is the biggest crowd in the history of Fenway Park?

A A doubleheader with the Yankees on September 22, 1935, drew 47,627 fans.

Q They called him "Double X" and "the Beast." This first baseman had already put up some huge numbers with the A's before being sold to Boston by Connie Mack for $150,000 in 1936. Who was he?

A Jimmie Foxx, who could still play baseball. In 1938, he batted .349, hit 50 home runs, and drove in 175 runs. That was his third American League MVP season. When he retired in 1946, only Babe Ruth had more homers.

Q Eddie Collins made a scouting trip to the West Coast in the late 1930s that turned out to be quite productive. Who did he sign?

A Ted Williams and Bobby Doerr.

He was Washington's primary second baseman in the 1920s. Even before his playing days were over, he had begun a very long career as a manager—the Senators from 1924 to 1928 (World Series champs in '24), the Tigers from 1929 to 1932, the Red Sox in 1934, the Senators again from 1935 to 1942, the Phillies in 1943, the Yankees in 1947 and 1948 (World Series champs in '47), the Senators yet again from 1950 to 1954, and the Tigers again in 1955 and 1956. He was also Boston's GM in 1959 and 1960. Who was this well-traveled individual?

A Bucky Harris.

Q Who are the Red Sox' top three pitchers in terms of complete games?

A Cy Young (275), Bill Dinneen (156), and George Winter (141)—three old-timers.

Q As part of an effort to rebuild his team in the mid-1930s, owner Tom Yawkey approved trades for what two brothers?

A Catcher Rick Ferrell came over from the Browns and his brother Wes, a pitcher, from the Indians. Rick caught 1,806 games, an AL record that stood until 1988 when Carlton Fisk passed it. And Wes was a great one, too. He won 193 games (peaking in 1935 with 25 victories). The two were sent, in a package deal, to Washington early in the 1937 season. The Ferrell brothers had very different personalities; Rick was jovial, while Wes was irascible in the extreme. Many times he was fined or suspended for refusing to leave a game, and sometimes he left without permission. In one instance, he was driven from the mound and proceeded to destroy the clubhouse, tear his uniform to shreds, and punch himself in the jaw.

Q In 1934, he earned a philosophy degree from Providence College, then played for the Tigers, Red Sox, and Indians, managed the Reds, Braves, and Indians, and scouted for another 28 years for the Mets, Yankees, Orioles, and Marlins. He was known for giving scouting reports that ranged from funny to brutal. Who was this baseball lifer?

A George "Birdie" Tebbetts. In his autobiography, Tebbetts recalled an umpire who, having just returned from World War II, suffered dizzy spells. The ump feared losing his job, so he asked Tebbetts, a catcher, for help with balls and strikes. He agreed and gave hand signals after each pitch.

Q This native of Reading, Pennsylvania, was an organization man through and through: He caught the eye of owner Tom Yawkey in 1935 and was a relief pitcher (and roommate of the cantankerous Ted Williams) before serving as a coach, assistant farm director, and scout in a career that spanned nearly seven decades. Name him.

A Charlie Wagner, also known as "Broadway" for his dapper dressing style.

Q What Texas-born third baseman came to the Red Sox from the A's in 1937 and led the team in batting for two years before heading to Detroit?

A Mike "Pinky" Higgins. He got back to Boston in 1946, just in time to help the team win the AL pennant and reach the World Series against St. Louis.

Q Higgins, who had been managing the Red Sox since 1955, was liked by most of his players perhaps because of his relaxed and nondemanding ways. But he was part and parcel of the team's resistance to integration, wasn't he?

A Indeed he was. Higgins was alleged to have said that no black player would be on any team he managed. Shortly after he stepped down in the middle of the 1959 season, Pumpsie Green was called up from the minors, ending the days of all-white major league baseball in Beantown. It would be unfair to put the onus entirely on the shoulders of Higgins, since he did not call all the shots. Owner Tom Yawkey and front office men Eddie Collins and Joe Cronin did that. At any rate, Higgins soon returned to the manager's job and was GM from 1963 to 1965. His record at both positions was mediocre at best.

Q Doc Cramer was 6' 2" and weighed 185 pounds, so he was not small, but he had very little power. Give an example of this fact.

A In both 1936 and 1938, he had more than 600 at-bats but did not hit a single home run.

Q Williams called Bobby Doerr "the silent captain of the Red Sox." What else is memorable about this fine second baseman?

A He went 3 for 5 on opening day in 1937, he had a .288 lifetime batting average, he made the All-Star team 10 times, and he once handled 414 straight chances without committing an error. Doerr hit .409 in the 1946 World Series and ended up with 223 home runs.

Q How many double plays did Doerr turn at second base in his career?

A A franchise-record 1,507, almost triple that of the next second baseman, Marty Barrett.

Q What was Ted Williams doing in 1937?

A The 18-year-old led the San Diego Padres to the Pacific Coast League championship.

Q What did the Red Sox pay the San Diego Padres for Williams after his second season in the minor leagues?

A $25,000. He spent one year tearing up the American Association with Minneapolis, and then it was time for the bigs.

Q Who are Lefty LeFebvre and Eddie Pelligrini?

A Both hit home runs for the Sox in their first major league plate appearances—the former in 1938 and the latter in 1946.

Q What happened at Yankee Stadium on May 30, 1938?

A New York beat Boston, 10-0, before a crowd of 83,533. During that game, the Yankees' Jake Powell was hit by a pitch thrown by Archie McCain of the Sox. Powell rushed the mound but was intercepted by Joe Cronin. The men had a particularly violent two-minute encounter before being stopped and ejected from the game. But they then met under the stands and continued their brawl until umpire Cal Hubbard (recently retired from pro football) put an end to it himself. Both were fined and suspended for 10 days.

Q How much did the St. Louis Browns fear first baseman Jimmie Foxx?

A Enough to walk him six straight times in a 12-8 Boston victory in 1938.

Q Who holds the team record for RBI in a season?

A Jimmie Foxx, who had 175 ribbies in 1938.

Q Two of Boston's greatest players drove in at least one run per game in 12 straight games. Who were they?

A Joe Cronin did it in 1939 and Ted Williams in 1942.

Q Name the Boston rookies who have hit three home runs in a game.

A Jim Tabor (1939), Norm Zauchin (1955), Joe Lahoud (1969), Fred Lynn (1975), and Trot Nixon (1999).

Ted Williams and batting coach Hugh Duffy, circa 1941. Williams would bat .406 that year, but Duffy had done even better for the Boston Braves a half-century earlier: .438, the all-time record.

Chapter Three
NO. 9

"When I walk down the street and meet people," Ted Williams once said, "I just want them to think, 'There goes the greatest hitter who ever lived.'" Although he did not match Ty Cobb's average or Babe Ruth's power, no one can doubt that Williams is on the short list of the best of the best batters of all time. He was talented, outspoken, demanding, iconoclastic, patriotic, and larger than life—just as Cobb and Ruth had been. Williams called hitting a pitched baseball "the hardest single feat in sports," and he obsessively spent time and effort on his craft. Despite losing nearly five years of his career to military service in World War II and the Korean War, "Teddy Ballgame" managed to hit 521 homers and compile a .344 average with 2,654 base hits.

But he wasn't perfect, not by any means. For one thing, he was slow afoot. This meant he could not beat out many infield hits, steal many bases, or hit many triples. It also limited his range in the outfield. His arm was fairly weak, too. He later regretted not striving harder to develop himself as a defensive player. Williams was the brash kid—and then elder statesman—who alternately dazzled and irked sportswriters, teammates, opponents, and fans. He and Cobb have been called the greatest players never to have won a championship, and he got into just one World Series: 1946, when he batted .200 (he had five singles). Even so, Joe DiMaggio later said of him, "He was absolutely the best hitter I ever saw."

Williams's unforgettable 1941 season, in which he batted .406, was overshadowed by DiMaggio's 56-game hitting streak that enthralled the nation through midsummer. Williams did, however, steal the spotlight from Joe D at the All-Star Game in Detroit. It was the bottom of the ninth inning with two men on and two out, the American League down by two runs, and 56,000 fans at Briggs Stadium clamoring for a three-run homer. Williams got a fastball from Claude Passeau of the Chicago Cubs and drove it over the right-field fence to win the game. He later called that hit the most thrilling of his career.

Q What transpired on April 20, 1939, at Yankee Stadium?

A The Red Sox showed off their prize rookie, Ted Williams, before 30,278 fans in the season opener, which had been delayed two days because of rain. Williams struck out twice and doubled.

Q What unusual thing happened on opening day, 1940?

A When President Franklin Roosevelt's ceremonial first pitch went awry and smashed a *Washington Post* camera. The chief executive was not, however, charged with a wild pitch.

Q His older brother (Vince) played two years with the crosstown Braves before moving on to four other teams. His younger brother (Joe) was among the finest players of all time for the Yankees. And he was quite a player himself. Who was he?

A Dom DiMaggio. An outfielder for the Red Sox from 1940 to 1953—minus three seasons for military service—he excelled as a leadoff batter, on defense, and on the basepaths. In 1949, his 34-game hitting streak ended with an outstanding catch by brother Joe.

Q Dom DiMaggio was as reserved and dignified as Joe, if not more so. What was his response one time when an umpire called him out on strikes?

A "I have never witnessed such incompetence in my life!"

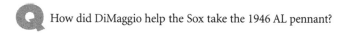

Q How did DiMaggio help the Sox take the 1946 AL pennant?

A When some of the other key players slumped in midseason, he helped keep Boston in the race. He batted .316 that year and scored the deciding run in Game 5 of the World Series.

Q Did Ted Williams ever pitch?

A As a matter of fact, he did. On August 24, 1940, his team was getting mauled by the Tigers so he was brought in for the final two innings. Williams gave up one run on three hits but struck out Rudy York on three pitches.

Q What was the controversy about the 1941 American League MVP award?

A Joe DiMaggio (with his 56-game hitting streak) won it, but Ted Williams (with his .406 average) had very strong credentials as well. The truth is, Williams alienated a lot of sportswriters, one of whom famously refused to put Williams on his top-ten list in 1941.

Q How did Williams do at home and on the road that year?

A He batted .428 at Fenway and .380 at other American League venues.

Q Who led the AL in 1942 in victories (22), complete games (22), strikeouts (113), and innings pitched (281)?

A Tex Hughson. This big right-hander had a hard fastball, an overhand curve, and didn't mind throwing inside. But arm and shoulder problems hastened his retirement in 1949.

Q Name the Red Sox' triple crown winners.

A Ted Williams (1942 and 1947) and Carl Yastrzemski (1967).

Q What two players have the most multi-homer games in team history?

A Ted Williams (37) and Jim Rice (35).

Q Summarize Williams's military service.

A He missed all of the 1943, 1944, and 1945 seasons, serving as a Marine Corps pilot. He flew propeller-driven aircraft. For most of the 1952 and 1953 seasons, Williams was back on active duty in Korea and transitioned to jet aircraft (once being lit up by enemy fire and crash-landing). Although these absences took nearly five years out of the heart of his career, significantly limiting his career totals, he did not complain about it—at least not in public.

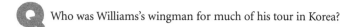

Q Who was Williams's wingman for much of his tour in Korea?

A John Glenn, later one of the seven original Mercury astronauts and the first American to orbit the earth. He also became a U.S. senator from Ohio. "We flew together quite a lot and got to know each other very well," said Glenn. "Ted was an excellent pilot and not shy about getting in there and mixing it up."

Q Who has the team record for pinch hits in a season?

A Joe Cronin had 18 in 1943. Dalton Jones, whose career with the Sox went from 1964 to 1969, has the career record of 55.

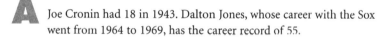

Q What outfielder had been terrorizing the American League for nearly two decades when he put on a Red Sox uniform in 1943? Hint: His real name was Aloys Szymanski.

A Al Simmons, who batted over .380 four times with the A's. He hung around a bit too long in an effort to reach 3,000 hits, falling short by 73.

Q What happened at Fenway Park in the spring of 1945?

A A Boston city councilman named Isadore Muchnick basically forced the Red Sox to offer a tryout to three black baseball players—Jackie Robinson, Sam Jethroe, and Marvin Williams. It was strictly a *pro forma* event; Tom Yawkey, Eddie Collins, and Joe Cronin sat and watched, stone-faced. They had no intention of offering a contract.

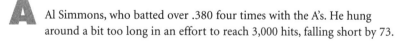

Q How did Cronin's playing career end?

A He broke his leg in a game at Yankee Stadium on April 19, 1945.

Q Name the Mississippian who pitched a two-hitter in his first game (in 1945) and was unscored upon the first 22 innings he was on the mound.

A David "Boo" Ferris. He was 21-10 as a rookie and 25-6 the next year, when the Sox got to the World Series against the Cardinals. By 1947, however, Ferris was suffering from arm problems and asthma, and his performance worsened. His promising career was over within three years. Ferris served as a pitching coach for the Red Sox between 1955 and 1959, and he also coached more than 1,000 games at Delta State University.

Q Due to World War II, there was no All-Star Game in 1945. What was done instead?

A A series of AL–NL exhibitions was held, including one at Fenway between the Sox and Braves. It drew 23,000 fans, plus nearly 1,000 servicemen, and raised $70,000 for war relief efforts in the Boston area. The Sox won, 8-1.

Q He embodied Red Sox players of the past who had fallen short of winning the World Series and was chosen, along with Carl Yastrzemski, to raise the flag up Fenway Park's center field flagpole after they finally won it in 2004. Who was this beloved figure?

A Shortstop Johnny Pesky. With 620 hits in his first three seasons (1942, 1946, and 1947), he was a very capable hitter. In the eighth inning of Game 7 of the '46 Series, Pesky caught the ball on a relay while the Cards' Enos Slaughter was motoring around the bases for the winning run. It has long been debated whether Pesky hesitated before throwing it home—too late. In 1963 and 1964, he had become manager but faced a tough task; the Sox were a second-rate team and some of the players defied his authority.

Q Back to the 1946 Series. If, in fact, Pesky hesitated before throwing home (and he concurred, calling himself "the goat"), a teammate was at fault, too. Who was he?

A Leon Culberson, who bobbled the ball hit to left-center field by Harry Walker. These two lapses, back to back, allowed Slaughter to make his famous "mad dash."

Q What part of Fenway is named after Pesky?

A The right field foul pole, known as Pesky's Pole. What few home runs he hit (just 17 in a 10-year career) were right down there in the corner.

Q What is the Lone Red Seat?

A On June 9, 1946, Joseph Boucher was attending a game between the Sox and Tigers. He was in the right field bleachers, in section 42, row 37, seat 21. In point of fact, he was napping until Ted Williams's 502-foot home run bounced off his head. The seat is painted red, distinct from its green counterparts.

Q What years has Boston hosted the All-Star Game?

A 1946 (the American League won, 12-0), 1961 (a 1-1 tie), and 1999 (the AL, 4-1).

Q The youngest of 14 children and a native of Durant, Oklahoma, this right-handed pitcher won one game in the 1946 World Series and finished his 14-year career with a 137-103 record. Identify him.

A Joe Dobson.

Q What is the longest winning streak in team history?

A The 1946 Red Sox won 15 straight games.

Q He excelled in basketball at New York University, served in World War II, and made it to the big leagues with the Red Sox in 1947. He played with five other clubs in a 10-year career, but he really made his mark as a manager of the Minnesota Twins. Who was he?

A Sam Mele, whose Twins lost to the Dodgers in the 1965 World Series. He later spent 25 years scouting for the Red Sox.

Q After a decade and a half of almost uninterrupted winning with the Yankees, what manager joined the Sox in 1948?

A Joe McCarthy. His teams came in second twice before he quit in the middle of the 1950 season.

Q Who did the Red Sox tie in the 1948 regular season, necessitating a one-game playoff?

A The Cleveland Indians. Their player-manager, Lou Boudreau, would manage the Sox from 1952 to 1954, but with little success.

Q And who won that playoff game at Fenway?

A The Tribe. The loss prevented an all-Beantown Series, as the Braves won the NL pennant.

Q Name the players who hit three consecutive home runs twice in one season.

A In 1948, Stan Spence, Vern "Junior" Stephens, and Ted Williams became the first trio to accomplish this feat twice in a single season.

Q This native of New Mexico was one of the best-hitting shortstops in major league history in a career that spanned 1941 to 1955. Identify him.

A Vern Stephens, who led the league in RBI three times. He was with the Red Sox from 1948 to 1952.

NO. 9

Q Who holds the team record for the longest hitting streak?

A Dom DiMaggio hit in 34 straight games in 1949. Tris Speaker (1912) and Nomar Garciaparra (1997) are next with 30.

Q What do you remember about Mel Parnell?

A He was a stylish left-handed pitcher, born and raised in New Orleans. Parnell spent his entire 10-year career with the Red Sox; his best season was 1949, when he went 25-7, had 27 complete games, and was the AL's starting pitcher in the All-Star Game. He won 18 each of the next two years.

Q When did Parnell toss a no-hitter?

A In 1956 against the White Sox. It was Boston's first no-hitter since Howard Ehmke did it back in '23.

Q Name the Boston pitchers who have led the AL in wins.

A Cy Young (33 in 1901, 32 in 1902, and 28 in 1903), Joe Wood (34 in 1912), Wes Ferrell (25 in 1935), Tex Hughson (22 in 1942), Mel Parnell (25 in 1949), Frank Sullivan (18 in 1955), Jim Lonborg (22 in 1967), Roger Clemens (24 in 1986 and 20 in 1987), Pedro Martinez (23 in 1999), and Curt Schilling (21 in 2004).

Q Since he didn't make it to the bigs until he was 31 years old, his teammates called him "Old Folks." His peak was with the Red Sox in 1949 when he won 23 games and lost 6, with six shutouts. Identify this man.

A Ellis Kinder. He moved to the bullpen in 1951 and was among the best relievers in the AL for five years.

Q Two players in team history have driven in 40 runs in a single month. Who are they?

A Ted Williams did it in May 1942 and June 1950, and Clyde Vollmer did it in July 1951.

Q Did the Red Sox and New York Yankees really discuss swapping Ted Williams and Joe DiMaggio?

A Yes they did. Tom Yawkey and Yankees GM Lee McPhail had a verbal agreement to do such a deal in 1949, but Yawkey wanted Yogi Berra as a throw-in. McPhail refused, and that was the end of it.

Q When did the Red Sox set the major league record for runs scored by one team?

A June 8, 1950, when they whacked the St. Louis Browns, 29-4.

Q Who holds the team record for grand-slam home runs?

A Ted Williams, who had 17 in his career. Next in line is Rico Petrocelli with nine.

Q He played every position except pitcher and catcher, led the AL in batting in 1950 with a .354 average, and was twice an All-Star. Name him.

A Billy Goodman, who later played with the Orioles, White Sox, and Houston Colt .45s. For a man whose career average over 16 major league seasons was .300, he has fallen into a remarkable obscurity.

Q Who was the Sox' first rookie of the year?

A First baseman Walt Dropo in 1950. A 6' 5" power hitter, he was as slow as molasses. Dropo had 34 home runs and 144 RBI for Boston that year, but he lost his magic soon thereafter. Traded to the Tigers (for whom he once had 12 consecutive hits, tying a major league record) in a nine-player deal in 1952, he also played for the White Sox, Reds, and Orioles before hanging it up in 1961.

Q Identify Boston's other rookies of the year.

A Don Schwall (1961), Carlton Fisk (1972), Fred Lynn (1975), and Nomar Garciaparra (1997).

Q What happened to Ted Williams in the 1950 All-Star Game?

A He suffered a fractured elbow while crashing into the left field wall at Comiskey Park. As a result, he played in only 89 games that season; the injury lingered two more years.

Q What rarity did Gil Coan of the Washington Senators accomplish against the Sox in a 1951 game?

A He hit two triples in one inning.

Q What occurred at Fenway on May 15, 1951?

A The Red Sox celebrated the 50-year anniversary of the founding of the American League. On hand were 29 old-timers who had played, managed, or been umpires that first year.

Q This University of Wyoming graduate did Red Sox radio and TV broadcasts from 1951 to 1966 before moving on to a national stage. Who was this man with the warm voice and easy style?

A Curt Gowdy.

Q How was Ted Williams honored on April 30, 1952?

A It was "Ted Williams Day" at Fenway Park—the day before he was to report for fighter pilot duty in the Korean War. He was 33 years old and not doing especially well. Although none dared say it out loud, the assumption was that he was playing in his final game. Williams hit a home run in his last at-bat that day.

Q The Boston Braves had moved to Milwaukee prior to the 1953 season. What effect did this have on the Red Sox' attendance?

A Oddly enough, it went down, from an average of 14,490 per game to 13,502. And the 1953 Red Sox won eight more games than had the '52 team.

Q Did Yawkey have a role in the Braves' move?

A Yes. He refused many requests to share Fenway Park and was involved in some behind-the-scenes action with the purpose of sending them on to Wisconsin.

Q What was the 4,000th win in franchise history?

A A 10-2 defeat of the A's on July 5, 1953.

Q Against what team did the Sox score 17 runs in one inning in a 1953 game?

A The Detroit Tigers.

A full house at Fenway Park.

Chapter Four
FUTILITY FOR FANS
AT FENWAY

Tom Yawkey had owned the Boston Red Sox for two decades, during which time they won a single AL pennant and no World Series titles. By the 1950s, they had slumped to mediocrity if not worse. Although the Braves had shifted to Milwaukee and the city was theirs alone, attendance stagnated. It seemed that the same 13,000 people attended each game.

And what did they see? Ted Williams, Dom DiMaggio, Johnny Pesky, Vern Stephens, and Ellis Kinder were all getting near the end of the line. An occasional prospect would brighten the scene momentarily, but the Red Sox were an afterthought to the Yankees, perennial winners of the flag. And if not New York, then Cleveland. The Indians—along with the Dodgers, the most fully integrated team in baseball—won 111 games in 1954; the Sox won a desultory 69. They had an opportunity to sign Willie Mays of the Birmingham Black Barons and chose not to do so.

Yawkey talked about expanding and modernizing Fenway Park, but he wanted local government to foot the bill and that was not going to happen. The players, who were generally among the best paid in the major leagues, just did not respond to the urgings of Yawkey, his front office, or managers Lou Boudreau, Pinky Higgins, and some whose names are barely remembered. By the late 1950s, Boston baseball fans knew their team would be no higher than the middle of the pack come season's end, so they turned a fond gaze toward Williams. Publicly and otherwise, some scribes had been urging him to quit for years, but he continued to come back and play remarkably well late in his career. Indeed, Williams's 1957 performance (.388 average, 38 home runs, 87 RBI, 96 runs scored, and 119 walks) remains, arguably, the best of any 39-year-old in the history of the game.

Q He caught 32 games for the 1954 Red Sox, but he will always be remembered for a passed ball in Game 4 of the 1941 World Series. Identify this man.

A Mickey Owen. His Brooklyn Dodgers lost the Series to the New York Yankees.

Q He was known as "the Golden Greek," had been a football star at Boston University, and was a first-round pick in the 1952 NFL draft. But the Red Sox outbid the Cleveland Browns for his services. Who was he?

A Harry Agganis. He played 119 games at first base in 1954 and was off to a fine start in 1955 when he died of a pulmonary embolism; some 10,000 mourners attended his wake. When BU opened a new athletic arena in 2005, it was named for Agganis.

Q What two Red Sox players have the most seasons of reaching base at least 300 times?

A Ted Williams (7) and Wade Boggs (6).

Q This Texan had spent most of his career playing third base for the Cincinnati Reds, but he was with Boston for most of 1954 and 1955, and would later help get big league baseball off the ground in Houston. Who was he?

A Grady Hatton. He was a front office executive with the Colt .45s and later managed them for two-and-a-half seasons as the Astros.

Q On June 12, 1954, this Indians ace got his 2,500th career strikeout and beat the Red Sox. Who was he?

A Bob Feller.

Q Handy with the glove, he was the first third baseman to lead the AL in games played, putouts, assists, double plays, and fielding percentage. All but one year of his career (1955–1966) was with Boston. Who was he?

A Frank Malzone. He remains among the Red Sox' all-time leaders in several offensive and defensive categories.

Q He was a talented athlete who played 17 years (with the Red Sox, Indians, Senators, Mets, and Angels) but suffered from bipolar disorder. Identify him.

A Jimmy Piersall. The list of his bizarre antics and fights—with opponents, teammates, fans, umpires, whoever—is lengthy. As an outfielder, Piersall's work drew comparisons to that of Joe DiMaggio, which is high praise indeed. His best year may have been 1956, when he batted .293, had 176 hits, and led the AL in doubles.

Q Williams was fined $5,000 by Red Sox management on August 7, 1956. Why?

A He spat at fans who had been booing him for misplaying a fly ball hit by Mickey Mantle in the 11th inning. It was actually Williams's third spitting incident within the past month.

Q He graduated from Villanova and, in a career that stretched from the late 1930s to the early 1960s, twice led the American League in batting. Who was this well-liked gentleman?

A Mickey Vernon, a stellar first baseman whose years with the Red Sox were 1956 and 1957. He later managed the Washington Senators.

Q He was the winning pitcher in the 1955 All-Star Game, helped the Milwaukee Braves win the World Series in 1957, and joined the Red Sox for the last three years of his career. Who was he?

A Gene Conley. What is most remarkable is that this 6' 8" player was adept at another sport—basketball. He had been an all-American at Washington State and played with the Boston Celtics and New York Knicks for six years. Conley remains the only man to win championships in both major league baseball and the NBA. His teammates included Hank Aaron, Bill Russell, Ted Williams, and Bob Cousy.

Q On May 22, 1957, the Red Sox set an American League record with four home runs in one inning. Who hit them?

A Gene Mauch, Ted Williams, Dick Gernert, and Frank Malzone. The homers came on just 16 pitches by the Indians' Cal McLish.

Q What did misogynistic sportswriters do at Fenway in 1957?

A They reaffirmed their decision to bar females from the male-only press box. The woman in question was Doris O'Donnell, a feature writer following the Cleveland Indians. When she asked Ted Williams for an interview, he rained epithets down upon her.

Q Boston baseball fans might well have been considering a jump into the Charles River in 1957 and 1958. Why?

A Their Red Sox finished third in the American League. The Braves (with Eddie Matthews, Hank Aaron, Warren Spahn, and other luminaries), meanwhile, had become wildly popular in Milwaukee. They were in the World Series both of those seasons, winning it once.

Q This native of Lufkin, Texas, was with the Red Sox from 1958 to 1962, hitting over .300 each year. Who was he?

A Pete Runnels, who played all four infield positions. His greatest day came on August 30, 1960, in a doubleheader against Detroit. He was 6-for-7 in the first game (with a game-winning RBI in the 15th inning) and 3-for-4 in the second, which tied a major league record for hits in a doubleheader. He also served as the Sox' interim manager the final 16 games of the 1966 season.

Q Who was Gladys Heffernan?

A Cronin's housekeeper. She was sitting in the stands at Fenway in September 1958 when an angry Ted Williams threw his bat into the crowd. The projectile hit her in the face.

Q Boston was the last major league team to integrate. Who were its first black players?

A Utility infielder Pumpsie Green joined the Sox in 1959 and was followed soon by pitcher Earl Wilson and center fielder Willie Tasby.

Q Green's brother was also an accomplished athlete. Who was he?

A Dallas Cowboys defensive back Cornell Green.

Q How was Green honored by the franchise 38 years later?

A He, along with Jackie Robinson's daughter, combined to throw out the opening pitches at Fenway Park on opening day, 1997.

Q On April 9, 1960, what happened at an exhibition game between the Indians and Red Sox in New Orleans?

A Black and white fans integrated the stands at City Park Stadium. Walter Bond hit two home runs in Cleveland's 12-8 win.

Q Name the only player who pinch-hit for both Ted Williams and Carl Yastrzemski.

A On September 20, 1960, Williams fouled a pitch off his foot and had to be taken out. Carroll Hardy stepped up to the plate and finished the at-bat by hitting into a double play. Less than a week later, he replaced Williams in left field in the legend's final game. "They booed me all the way out and cheered him all the way in," Hardy later recalled. On May 31, 1961, he pinch-hit for Yaz. And if that were not enough, Hardy (who had played football with the San Francisco 49ers) once pinch-hit for Roger Maris when they were teammates with the Kansas City Athletics.

Q What was Ted Williams's final at-bat?

A On September 28, 1960, the Sox were playing Baltimore at Fenway. He hit a pitch 450 feet into the right-centerfield seats. Despite a standing ovation, he remained in the dugout—obstinate to the end.

Q What famous essay did author John Updike pen about Williams's last game?

A "Hub Fans Bid Kid Adieu," which appeared in *The New Yorker* magazine on October 22, 1960.

Q Who was the first person to play in both the Rose Bowl and the World Series?

A Jackie Jensen. First, his football achievements: Jensen was an all-America halfback at the University of California in 1948. The Bears lost that season's Rose Bowl contest to Northwestern. But Jensen also excelled at baseball, leading Cal to the first College World Series championship. After one year of minor league ball, he was with the Yankees in the 1950 Series against the Phillies. With the arrival of Mickey Mantle, Jensen's value dropped and so he was traded to Washington and from there to Boston.

Q Jensen, American League MVP with the Sox in 1958 (.286 batting average, 35 homers, 122 RBI), retired prematurely. Why?

A He had an aversion to air travel. Jensen could have played another five years, but the panic attacks at airports and inside planes were too much, so he quit.

Q He rose through the ranks to become GM of the club twice—1961–1962 and 1965–1977—and has been credited with reviving the Red Sox from near-irrelevance with the '67 "impossible dream" group. Who was he?

A Dick O'Connell.

Q O'Connell, fired by Jean Yawkey in 1977 after the death of her husband, was back on the scene six years later. What happened?

A Jean Yawkey had sold part of the club to a group headed by Haywood Sullivan, but in 1983 (the Sox' first losing season since 1966) one of the general partners, Edward "Buddy" LeRoux, attempted a *coup d'etat*—supposedly exercising an option in their partnership agreement. He unveiled O'Connell as his choice to lead the team. Yawkey and Sullivan filed suit and prevailed a year later, after the revelation of many sordid details.

Q What was Sullivan's background?

A He had played football and baseball at the University of Florida. He was a third-string catcher for the Sox in the late 1950s, but had a modicum of success with Kansas City and managed the A's to a last-place finish in 1965. Sullivan joined the Red Sox front office soon thereafter and eventually became GM. He parlayed $100,000—using his home as collateral—into $33 million when he sold his share of the team in 1993.

Q Didn't Sullivan's son play for the Sox?

A He sure did—from 1982 to 1987. Marc Sullivan was a catcher, too, and he was no better than his dad. He played in 137 games and batted just .186.

Q Among Red Sox opponents, who has the most home runs at Fenway Park?

A The record is shared by two Yankees—Babe Ruth and Mickey Mantle (38). Ruth also had 11 at home during his six seasons with the Sox.

Q What ex–Red Sox pitcher had been a basketball star at the University of Oklahoma?

A Don Schwall. His career got off to a roaring start in 1961 (15-7 and AL rookie of the year), but he was soon shipped to Pittsburgh and from there to Atlanta.

 He was a finesse pitcher who won 114 games in a career that lasted 11 years—the first eight with Boston. Who was he?

A Bill Monbouquette.

Q What else did Monbouquette do for the Sox?

A He struck out 17 batters against the Senators in 1961, threw a no-hitter against the White Sox in 1962, and had three one-hit games.

Q What Boston right-hander was on the mound at Yankee Stadium on the last day of the 1961 season and gave up Roger Maris's 61st home run?

A Tracy Stallard. Later with the Mets and Cards, Stallard had this to say about Maris's record-breaker: "I have nothing to be ashamed of. He hit 60 others, didn't he?"

Q Name the erudite sportscaster who did Red Sox games from 1961 to 1992.

A Ned Martin, who also covered pro football with the Boston Patriots and college games with Harvard, Yale, and Dartmouth. Martin was behind the microphone for some of the most unforgettable moments in franchise history, using the signature exclamation, "Mercy!"

Q Who was Earl Wilson?

A This big right-handed pitcher was first called up to the Red Sox on July 31, 1959. Three years later, at Fenway, he threw a no-hitter against the Los Angeles Angels and hit one of his 35 career home runs.

Q What fastballing pitcher had won a Cy Young Award and a World Series MVP with the Yankees before playing one last season with the Sox in 1963?

A Bob Turley.

Q What Boston manager did Stuart take particular pleasure in tormenting?

A Johnny Pesky.

Q What Red Sox pitcher, nicknamed "the Monster," saved 24 games in 1962 and 25 in 1963?

A Dick Radatz, who stood 6' 6" and weighed 230 pounds. He threw two innings in the 1963 All-Star game, striking out Willie Mays, Dick Groat, Duke Snider, Willie McCovey, and Julian Javier. Radatz developed arm trouble by 1965 and finished up with the Indians, Cubs, Tigers, and Expos.

Q He hit 66 home runs in one season in the minors, helped the Pirates win the 1960 World Series, and was with the BoSox for two years. But he might be entirely forgotten if not for the rather cruel nickname pinned on him—"Dr. Strangeglove." To whom do we refer?

A Dick Stuart, of course. He had his best season in 1963 with Boston, hitting 42 homers, driving in 118 runs, and committing 29 errors, which was also a personal record. Stuart was a fashion plate, a jovial guy, and a night owl who sometimes drove his managers nuts. It has been suggested that he was really a *careless* fielder more than a truly bad one.

Q This Brooklyn native played his entire career (1963–1976) with the Red Sox. In 1969, he set what was then a record for shortstops by hitting 40 dingers. Who was he?

A Rico Petrocelli. With the acquisition of Luis Aparicio, he moved easily to third base. Petrocelli hit two home runs in Game 6 of the 1967 World Series against St. Louis and played well in the '75 Fall Classic against Cincinnati.

Q He was the ultimate utility man—able to adequately cover all spots in the infield and outfield—and won a World Series title with the Milwaukee Braves before spending four seasons in the Hub City. Who was he?

A Felix Mantilla. He loved hitter-friendly Fenway Park so much, he hit 30 home runs in 1964.

Q Dave Morehead was having a pretty awful year in 1965, leading the American League in losses (18). But he had one very good moment. What was it?

A On September 16 of that year, he threw a no-hitter against the Cleveland Indians.

Q How bad were things at Fenway Park in 1965?

A Pretty awful. The Sox were perennial losers, the stadium was in disrepair, and attendance had fallen to an average of 8,052 per game. Owner Tom Yawkey was threatening to move the team if things did not improve.

Q How many people showed up for the '65 season finale?

A Fewer than 500 souls were at Fenway to see the Yankees take an 11-5 win, with Whitey Ford getting the "W."

Q This right-handed reliever spent six years with Milwaukee at the beginning of his career, five with San Francisco at the end, and sandwiched in between were stints with Houston, Cleveland, Boston, the Chicago White Sox, and the Tigers. Identify him if you can.

A Don McMahon. One of his top performances with Boston came on June 4, 1966, against the Yankees. He pitched four innings of shutout relief, allowed one walk and no hits, and helped the team to a 6-3 win in 16 innings.

Q This TV and radio broadcaster handled the games of the Cleveland Browns from 1952 to 1965, the Indians from 1954 to 1963, the Red Sox from 1965 to 1974, the Reds from 1975 to 1978, and then was back with Boston for another decade. Who was he?

A Ken Coleman.

Q What notable thing did Ted Williams say in his Hall of Fame induction speech in 1966?

A He called for recognition of great Negro Leaguers like Satchel Paige and Josh Gibson. Williams's statement was instrumental in the Hall of Fame eventually inducting those two and others.

Q Name the seven Red Sox pitchers who have started in an All-Star Game.

A Lefty Grove (1936), Mel Parnell (1949), Bill Monbouquette (1960), Dennis Eckersley (1982), Roger Clemens (1986), Pedro Martinez (1999), and Derek Lowe (2002).

Roger Clemens early in his BoSox career.

Chapter Five
CLOSE, BUT NOT QUITE, IN '67, '75, AND '86

The beneficent Tom Yawkey was still the owner of the franchise, and his cronies were still in charge in the early 1960s. A "country-club" atmosphere prevailed, and postgame boozing was not at all unheard of. There was one promising young player, outfielder Carl Yastrzemski, but really the team was just rocking along. Attendance was even worse than in the 1950s—no surprise, given the dull, losing (eight straight years under .500) teams on display at Fenway Park. But change, long overdue, was coming. General manager Dick O'Connell swept out much of the dead wood and brought in baseball people, one of whom was Dick Williams.

As a player, Williams had scratched out a 13-year career with Brooklyn, Baltimore, Cleveland, Kansas City, and Boston. Prior to the 1967 season, he signed a one-year contract with the Red Sox. Williams quickly installed a my-way-or-the-highway approach and got surprising results—securing the first pennant in 21 years. They extended the highly favored St. Louis Cardinals to seven games in the World Series before falling. An invigorated farm system had become more colorblind, the organization was shedding its culture of losing, and a new generation of fans had come to appreciate the BoSox.

Exhilarating as the 1967 season had been, however, Boston did not win it all. Nor did they overcome the Cincinnati Reds in the 1975 World Series (which some baseball historians have credited with sparking a revival of enthusiasm for the game) or the New York Mets 11 years later. Yaz was gone by then, but he had been replaced by a hitting machine named Wade Boggs. They came close, but please, let's remember that Bill Buckner's famous error at first base took place in Game 6 (not Game 7) of that Series. The Sox had another opportunity to win and they did not. Billy B got too much static about that for too long.

Q Why was O'Connell able to take control of the franchise in the mid-1960s?

A Yawkey was spending more time on his South Carolina estate and was essentially out of the way. But he was not gone for long.

Q What event has been called the birth of Red Sox Nation?

A When Dick Williams's team won 10 straight on the road in '67 and returned to an exuberant welcome from 10,000 fans at Logan Airport.

Q Billy Rohr's career got off to a most promising start. What happened?

A Rohr must have made quite an impression with manager Dick Williams and the Boston coaching staff because he was given the opening day assignment on April 14, 1967, against New York. His counterpart for the Yankees was Whitey Ford, making his 432nd career start. Nevertheless, Rohr retired the first 26 batters before Elston Howard got a hit, so he settled for a shutout. He beat the Yankees again in his next start, but that was it—he never won another game for Boston.

Q Did Rohr pitch for any other teams?

A He was with Cleveland briefly in 1968, kicked around the minors for a while, and was soon out of baseball. Still, some observers thought Rohr's amazing opening day performance was a catalyst for the Red Sox' winning the AL pennant.

Q This hometown hero started playing for the Sox in 1964 and looked like a future Hall of Famer until he was beaned on August 18, 1967. Who was he?

A Tony Conigliaro. In a home game against the Angels, he was facing Jack Hamilton when a wild pitch broke his left cheekbone and severely damaged his left retina. Eighteen months later, though, "Tony C" was back, hitting 20 home runs with 82 RBI in 141 games, and his numbers were even better in 1970. But problems with his eyesight never went away completely. He played with the Angels and came back to Boston before retiring in 1975. Conigliaro suffered a heart attack in 1982 and was in a coma for eight years before dying.

Q Perhaps no player, next to Carl Yastrzemski, contributed more to the Red Sox' run to the 1967 AL pennant than this right-handed pitcher. Who was he?

A Jim Lonborg. He played for 15 years (including with Milwaukee and Philadelphia), but '67 was undoubtedly his best. He went 22-9 with 246 strikeouts, and threw a one-hitter against St. Louis in the World Series.

Q Lonborg, in 1967, was Boston's first Cy Young Award winner. Who are the others?

A Roger Clemens (1986, 1987, and 1991) and Pedro Martinez (1999 and 2000).

Q What non-baseball injury derailed Lonborg's very promising career?

A It was an off-season skiing accident in which he wrecked his knee.

Q This South Carolinian was obtained from Kansas City late in the 1967 season to replace the injured Tony Conigliaro. He helped the Sox win the pennant, hit 35 homers the next year, and led the league in RBI with 109. Who was he?

A Ken "Hawk" Harrelson. He later attempted to make it as a pro golfer, worked as the White Sox' GM in 1986 (and is remembered primarily for firing manager Tony La Russa), and has been with their TV broadcast team since 1991.

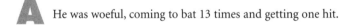

Q How did Harrelson do in the '67 Series?

A He was woeful, coming to bat 13 times and getting one hit.

Q He had been a basketball player at Oklahoma State and earned most of his major league recognition as a great field/no hit guy with the Orioles. But the Sox acquired him early in the 1967 season, and he did his part for the AL champs. Who was he?

A Jerry Adair.

Q He was a switch-hitting rookie outfielder when the Sox made their run to the World Series in 1967, who twice led the AL in homers and once in batting average. Name him.

A Reggie Smith, who later went on to play for St. Louis, Los Angeles, and San Francisco.

Q Name the colorful first baseman who collected eight Gold Gloves and tied a rookie record by playing 162 games with the Red Sox in 1966.

A George "Boomer" Scott. He hit 27 home runs in '66 and batted .303 in 1967. The next year, however, his offense took a tumble as he hit just .171, establishing a record for the lowest batting average for a first baseman who took part in 100 games. He later played with the Brewers, Royals, and Yankees.

Q He was with the Sox from 1967 to 1971, but not until he went to the Yankees did he truly flourish. Who was this fine relief pitcher?

A Sparky Lyle, who helped New York win back-to-back World Series in 1977 and 1978. He later logged time with the Rangers, Phillies, and White Sox.

Q It was April 27, 1968. After almost being scratched due to a sore throat, this pitcher no-hit the Red Sox, 6-0, after a rain delay of one hour and 23 minutes at Baltimore's Memorial Stadium. Who was he?

A Tom Phoebus. He also went 2-for-4 at the plate, scored, and drove in a run for the Orioles.

Q This native of Puerto Rico was with the Milwaukee Braves when they won the 1957 title and tossed a pair of no-hitters for the Chicago White Sox in 1962. He was well past his prime when Boston had him for parts of 1968 and 1969. Who was he?

A Juan Pizarro.

Q What did Ted Williams do after retiring as a player?

A He fished a lot, he managed the Washington Senators/Texas Rangers for three years, and he wrote a book, *The Science of Hitting*, which only served to further raise the esteem in which he was held.

Q How long did Dick Williams stay in Boston?

A Not long. By 1971, he was in Oakland, making the A's into the winners of two championships.

Q Who was one of Tony Conigliaro's teammates in 1969 and 1970?

A His brother, Billy. On July 4, 1970, they both homered in a game against the Indians. They hit a total of 54 that year.

Q He played in 2,599 major league games (every single one at shortstop) for the White Sox, Orioles, and Red Sox. In 1984, he became the first native of South America to reach the Hall of Fame. Who was he?

A Luis Aparicio. His game, it must be admitted, had drastically declined by the time he got to Boston in 1971.

Q He played basketball and baseball at the University of New Hampshire but chose to focus on the latter as a pro. Who might he be?

A Catcher Carlton Fisk. He played a smattering of games for the Red Sox in 1969 and 1971 before his first full season, in 1972. Rookie of the year, he took control of the position and never looked back in a career that lasted 23 seasons. Fisk, the original "Pudge," signed a free-agent contract with Chicago in 1981 and ran the White Sox' show for 12 more years. No player has ever caught as many games (2,226) as he did. He was held in such high regard by his two former clubs that Fisk got an honorary ring after the Red Sox' World Series victory in 2004 and one from the White Sox the next year.

Q What is the "Fisk Pole"?

A Let's go back to the 12th inning of Game 6 of the '75 Series. Fisk lined Pat Darcy's sinker off the left field foul pole and into the stands while urging the ball to stay fair as he danced down the first base line—an enduring image in the history of baseball. In 2005, the Red Sox honored Fisk by naming the pole after him.

Q This 1963 AL rookie of the year for the White Sox still had some gas in the tank when he joined Boston six years later. Who was he?

A Gary Peters, the winner of 30 games in 1970 and 1971.

Q On a Wednesday afternoon in the summer of 1973, the Red Sox and Yankees met at Fenway Park. What memorable event transpired?

A Thurman Munson, coming home on a suicide squeeze, bowled over Carlton Fisk, who held onto the ball for the out. Munson punched Fisk, who countered with some strong shots of his own. Both dugouts emptied, and both catchers were ejected. The Sox won, 3-2.

Q One more question about Fisk. How many home runs did he hit after age 40?

A He had what was then a major league record of 72—although that's when he was playing for the White Sox.

CLOSE, BUT NOT QUITE, IN '67, '75, AND '86

Q What left-handed pitcher went 13-2 for Boston in 1973?

A Rogelio (Roger) Moret. He did quite well in 1975, too, going 14-3.

Q Who holds Boston's record for the most stolen bases in a season?

A Tommy Harper, who swiped 54 in 1973. Tris Speaker's record of 52 had stood since 1912.

Q This Puerto Rican, known as "the Baby Bull," had been NL rookie of the year with the Giants in 1958 and was MVP with the Cardinals in 1967. He had a late-career resurgence with Boston in 1973. Who was he?

A Orlando Cepeda. He took advantage of the new designated hitter rule by playing in 142 games for the Sox, batting .289, and hitting 20 homers. Cepeda's conviction for participating in a drug-running operation in San Juan delayed his election to the Hall of Fame, but it finally happened in 1999.

Q This pitcher had a most unusual delivery—turning away from home plate briefly before throwing—but it surely worked. Who was he? Hint: He won 81 games for Boston between 1973 and 1976.

A "El Tiante"—Luis Tiant. He was one of the best and most beloved pitchers in modern Red Sox history. Tiant, whose father was a legendary player back in Cuba, won two games in the 1975 World Series.

Q What fastballer had 19 strikeouts against the Red Sox in a 4-2 win in 1974?

A Nolan Ryan of the California Angels.

Q Describe what happened to the Sox in the final weeks of the 1974 season.

A Darrell Johnson's team squandered an eight-game division lead and finished seven behind Baltimore.

Q They called this shortstop "the Rooster," and he was a fan favorite in Boston from 1974 to 1980. Identify him.

A Rick Burleson. A four-time All-Star, he also played with Baltimore and California.

Q This journeyman outfielder and designated hitter spent time with six franchises (two stints in Boston) from 1969 to 1980. Name him.

A Bernie Carbo, who smacked a dramatic pinch-hit homer in Game 6 of the 1975 World Series.

Q What did pitcher Dick Drago do for the Sox in 1975?

A He saved 15 regular season games, then two in the ALCS against Oakland. He pitched three scoreless innings in Game 6 of the World Series against Cincinnati, won on Carlton Fisk's home run.

Q He managed the Sox from 1974 until mid-1976 when the AL champs were slumping more than his bosses could bear. Who was he?

A Darrell Johnson, later the skipper with Seattle and Texas.

Q He and fellow rookie Jim Rice were called "the Gold Dust Twins" in 1975, and what a year he had: a .331 batting average, the Gold Glove Award for his stellar play in center field, rookie of the year, and MVP. Who was he?

A Fred Lynn. Although he enjoyed success in the remainder of his 17-year career, Lynn had trouble—due to nagging injuries—duplicating what he had done in '75. He also played with the Angels, Orioles, Tigers, and Padres before hanging it up.

Q What had Lynn done in college?

A His University of Southern California teams won the College World Series three times.

Q What Red Sox player won the first of his eight Gold Gloves in 1976?

A Dwight Evans. "Dewey," as he was known, mastered Fenway's tricky right-field corner early in his 20-year career (all but one with Boston) and had the best arm of any American League outfielder.

Q Was Evans always a wiz with the bat?

A No, his performance improved markedly in the second half of his career. Hitting coach Walt Hriniak gave him a balanced batting stance and helped transform him into a powerful slugger, as Evans finished his career with 385 home runs. By the way, only Carl Yastrzemski played more games in a Red Sox uniform.

Q Who, exactly, is Ben Mondor?

A General manager Haywood Sullivan prevailed upon Mondor to buy the Triple-A Pawtucket Red Sox in 1977. Things seemed hopeless, but he and president Mike Tamburro somehow succeeded; it became a model minor league franchise. His team drew more than 11 million fans during Mondor's tenure, and he was inducted into the Red Sox Hall of Fame in 2004.

Q What major league record did the Indians and Red Sox establish in 1977 at Fenway Park?

A The Tribe scored 13 runs and the Red Sox 6 in the eighth inning of their game—the most runs ever scored by both teams in one inning. Cleveland won, 19-9.

Q On July 4, 1977, in a game with the Blue Jays, six Boston players hit a total of eight home runs. Identify these men.

A Fred Lynn (2), George Scott (2), Bernie Carbo, Butch Hobson, Jim Rice, and Carl Yastrzemski.

Q This pitcher was with Cleveland (where he threw a no-hitter against the Angels) before coming to Boston in a trade. In 1978 and 1979, he had his best years as a starter, winning 37 games. Who was he?

A Dennis Eckersley. He fell into relative mediocrity the next few seasons, both for the Red Sox and White Sox. A trade to Oakland—his hometown—in 1987, along with some alcohol rehab, brought him back to the top. Manager Tony LaRussa made Eckersley a reliever, and he was one of the best ever, winning the AL Cy Young Award and MVP in 1992. No longer the brash young flamethrower of his early years, he finished up with Boston in 1998 and is now part of the Sox' broadcast team.

Q What are the current dimensions of Fenway Park?

A 310 feet to the left field line, 379 to left-center, 390 to center, 420 to right-center, and 302 to the right field line. It is 60 feet from home plate to the backstop.

Q Besides the Red Sox, who have been the other sports tenants there?

A The Boston Braves (1914–1915), the Boston Redskins of the National Football League (1933–1936), the Boston Yanks of the NFL (1944–1948), the Boston Patriots of the American Football League (1963–1967), and the Boston Beacons of the North American Soccer League (1968). Boston College and Boston University have also played some football games there.

Q What is the mailing address of the Red Sox' home?

A 4 Yawkey Way, Boston, MA 02215.

Q Who played quarterback for Bear Bryant at Alabama before embarking on an eight-year major league baseball career?

A Third baseman Butch Hobson, whose best year was 1977 when he hit 30 home runs and had 112 RBI.

Q Was Hobson an adept defensive player?

A Not in the least. Hobson (Sox manager from 1992 to 1994) had a whopping 43 errors in 1978.

Q He was the 1978 American League MVP, played all 16 years of his career in a Boston uniform, and had a .298 average and 382 homers. Who was he?

A Jim Rice. He also played quite well in the 1986 Series. There is no more vigorous long-term debate than whether or not Rice belongs in the Hall of Fame. He did tail off quite a bit in his final six seasons, he hit into a lot of double plays, and he was an average fielder, at best. But his stats look good in comparison with those of the 19 left fielders in the Hall.

Q This infielder was beaned twice in his baseball career but persevered, playing 12 years with the Dodgers (both in Brooklyn and LA), Cubs, Mets, Reds, and Senators. He is best known today as a manager and coach, however. Identify him.

A Don Zimmer. He was the Sox' skipper when Bucky Dent of the Yankees hit his homer over the Green Monster in 1978 and was a bench coach during New York's run of four World Series titles in the late 1990s.

Q What was the Boston Massacre?

A That name was given to the Yankees' four-game sweep of the Red Sox in early September 1978 (by the scores of 15-3, 13-2, 7-0, and 7-4), a crushing series of defeats for Don Zimmer's team.

Q Bucky Dent's homer against the Red Sox in a playoff game is among the more memorable events in franchise history. What were the circumstances when the New York shortstop bopped the ball over Fenway Park's Green Monster?

A The Yankees had been 14 games behind the Red Sox in July, but they began to win and Boston began to lose. Then the Sox won their last eight games, tying the Yanks and setting up a one-game playoff. It was the seventh inning, a fierce wind was blowing out to left field, and Mike Torrez threw the fateful pitch. BoSox fans still rue the day— October 2, 1978.

Q He wore the Red Sox uniform briefly (84 games) in a career that spanned 1966 to 1984. He later went on to be the GM for the Astros and Yankees, then a vice-president in major league baseball. Who was he?

A Bob Watson. He holds the distinction of being the first player to hit for the cycle in both leagues—for Houston in 1977 and Boston in 1979.

Q Who was the opposing pitcher when Carl Yastrzemski got his 3,000th hit on September 12, 1979?

A Jim Beattie of the Yankees.

Q And while we're at it, when did Yaz play in his 3,000th game?

A May 25, 1981, against the Indians. The only others to have done that are Ty Cobb, Stan Musial, and Hank Aaron.

Q Yazstremski played what other positions besides left field?

A He was in center most of the 1964 season, as Tony Conigliaro was in left. He also played 765 games at first base, 411 games as a designated hitter, and 31 games at third.

Q Why in the world was Yazstremski put at third base, and how did he do?

A It was manager Eddie Kasko's idea (in the 1973 season), and the experiment was less than successful; the error-prone Yaz was soon shifted back to first.

Q Where did Roger Clemens attend college?

A The University of Texas. He was 25-7 in two seasons with the Longhorns, winners of the 1983 College World Series.

Q They didn't call him "Spaceman" for nothing, but he was a fine pitcher with a career record of 119-90. Who was he?

A Bill Lee, naturally. He had pitched at USC and got to the major leagues within 18 months. Unafraid to tell management—or the media—what he thought, he inevitably clashed with old-school baseball men like manager Don Zimmer. But Lee had no shortage of supporters among fans in Boston and Montreal, where he played for four seasons after leaving the Sox; in fact, he had a cult following of sorts and is still good for a quote if he can be found on his organic farm in Vermont.

Q Two rarities happened at Comiskey Park on June 16, 1979. What were they?

A In an 11-5 defeat of the White Sox, Rick Burleson had an inside-the-park homer and Carl Yastrzemski got his 1,000th extra-base hit.

Q This first baseman, a native of Camaguey, Cuba, was a major contributor to Cincinnati's Big Red Machine that won the World Series twice in the mid-1970s. His last really good year was with Boston in 1980 when he hit .275 and had 25 homers. Who was he?

A Tony Perez, who was a manager of no distinction with the Reds (1993) and Marlins (2001).

Q What did diminutive Fred Patek do against the Red Sox on June 20, 1980?

A The 5' 5" shortstop hit three home runs to help the California Angels beat Boston, 20-2.

Q How did Carlton Fisk do in his first game for the White Sox after leaving Boston in 1981?

A He hit a three-run homer in the eighth inning to lead Chicago to a 5-3 win over his former teammates at Fenway Park.

Q What Red Sox third baseman led the AL in batting (.336) in 1981?

A Carney Lansford. With the emergence of Wade Boggs, he was sent to Oakland where he played for another decade.

Q Who was known as "Oil Can?"

A That would be Dennis Boyd, a pitcher blessed with an irrepressible personality. He played from 1982 to 1991, all but the last two years with the Sox. Boyd got the nickname from his beer-drinking days in Meridian, Mississippi.

Q What relief pitcher had 33 saves and an ERA of 2.45 for the Sox in 1983?

A Bob "the Steamer" Stanley. A sinkerball specialist who spent his entire 13-year career with Boston, he is the franchise's all-time leader in appearances with 637.

Q What happened at Fenway on October 2, 1983?

A It was the last day of the season and the last game of Carl Yastrzemski's career. This man, who had made the Red Sox matter again, got a much-deserved, six-minute ovation in pregame ceremonies. He finished with 3,419 hits, the most in club history.

Q What Venezuelan-born player led the AL in homers (43), RBI (123), and total bases (339) in 1984?

A Tony Armas. From 1980 to 1985, no American Leaguer hit more home runs.

Q Who was New York's starter at Fenway on opening day in 1985?

A That was 46-year-old Phil Niekro. He was the oldest pitcher since 1931 to start an opening game. Boston chased him after four innings, and behind the pitching of Oil Can Boyd he coasted to a 9-2 win.

Q In Game 5 of the 1986 ALCS, the California Angels were one pitch from going to the World Series. It was the top of the ninth inning when this player hit a two-run homer off Donnie Moore, putting Boston ahead, 6-5. The Angels tied it up in the bottom of the ninth but the same batter won the game in the 11th with a sacrifice fly. Identify him.

A Dave Henderson. He would later help the Oakland A's win three AL pennants and one World Series title. Moore, by the way, pitched two more years but could never shake the sense of depression that resulted from Henderson's big homer. On July 18, 1989, beset with alcoholism, drug abuse, and financial and marital worries, he shot his wife and then killed himself. (It should be noted that the '86 ALCS did not end with that game. The Angels were still ahead, 3-2, but lost their last two at Fenway, sending the Sox on to face the Mets in the Series.)

Q What Boston player had an AL-record 23 game-winning RBI in 1986?

A Mike Greenwell.

Q In 1986, this shortstop became the first major leaguer in 40 years to score six runs in a game as the Red Sox routed the Indians, 24-5. Who was he?

A Spike Owen.

Q Don Baylor, designated hitter with the Sox in 1986 and 1987, racked up an unusual record. What was it?

A A power hitter who often crowded the plate, Baylor did not mind getting hit by pitches; he owns the record with 267. By the time he retired, Baylor had 338 homers, 2,135 hits, and 285 stolen bases. He played in three straight World Series—1986 with the Sox, 1987 with the Twins, and 1988 with the A's—and later managed the Colorado Rockies and Chicago Cubs.

Q This Boston player led the AL in batting average five times in the 1980s and won two Gold Gloves at third base. Identify him.

A Wade Boggs. He was primarily a singles hitter, but in 1987 when he was up for a new contract he stroked 24 home runs. Boggs finished his 18-year career as a member of the Tampa Bay Devil Rays, with 3,010 hits and an average of .328. His station, in the eyes of sabermetricians and baseball historians, has risen due to his high on-base percentage.

Q Boggs set a team record for multi-hit games in 1985. What was it?

A He had at least two hits in 72 games. He also had at least 200 hits in seven straight seasons (1983–1989).

Q Boggs's 240 hits in 1985 broke whose team record?

A That of Tris Speaker, who had 222 back in 1912, albeit playing the 154-game schedule.

Q Bill Buckner made a rather large error in Game 6 of the 1986 World Series. But what happened to his career after that?

A Buckner played from 1969 to 1990 (with the Dodgers, Cubs, Red Sox [twice], Angels, and Royals), compiling some very nice stats. He led the NL in batting in 1980 (.324), was a fine base-stealer early on, and seldom struck out. And let the record show that Buckner was not error prone.

Q What pair of teammates holds the record for homering in the same game?

A Dwight Evans and Jim Rice did it 56 times between 1974 and 1989.

Q Who won two games in the 1986 World Series and gave up just three singles in six innings of Game 7?

A Bruce Hurst. He and Roger Clemens combined to make a formidable one-two punch in the mid- and late 1980s. Hurst later pitched with the Padres, Rockies, and Rangers.

Q This 6' 5" Texan came over from the Mets and was Boston's bullpen ace in the last half of the 1986 season. Who was he?

A Calvin Schiraldi. Good as he was then, he self-destructed in the postseason. Schiraldi lost Game 4 of the ALCS to the Angels and Games 6 and 7 of the World Series to the Mets. He is the only pitcher in major league history to hold that dubious distinction.

Q How do Fenway's clubhouses compare with those to be found in most other baseball stadiums?

A Small and none too fancy—that's the best way to put it. Like Fenway itself, its clubhouse compensates for the lack of modern amenities with old-fashioned charm and a sense of history. The tunnels leading to the dugouts are often wet, there are seats with obstructed views (or that don't face in the ideal direction), and more than a few rats call Fenway home. Antiseptic, it's not.

Q What other famous athletic event passes by Fenway Park every April?

A Mile 25 of the Boston Marathon is right outside on Lansdowne Street.

Q Roger Clemens won three Cy Young Awards with the Red Sox. When were they?

A 1986 (a record of 24-4, a 2.48 ERA, and 238 strikeouts), 1987 (20-9, 2.97, and 256), and 1991 (18-10, 2.62, and 241). Of course, he also won the award with the Toronto Blue Jays in 1997 and 1998, the New York Yankees in 2001, and the Houston Astros in 2004.

Q What did Clemens do on April 29, 1986?

A As 13,414 shivering fans at Fenway Park looked on, he struck out 20 Seattle Mariners and thus set a new major league record for a nine-inning game.

Q He won 311 games in his 20-season career, but only the last five were with the Sox. To what fine pitcher do we refer?

A Tom Seaver, the 1967 NL rookie of the year (with the New York Mets) and three-time Cy Young Award winner.

Johnny Damon, one of the heroes with the 2004 World Series champs.

Chapter Six
HOPE AND FAITH REWARDED

The 1988 and 1990 Red Sox got into the playoffs, but they went a combined 0-8 against Oakland. In the ALCS five years later, they were swept again—this time by Cleveland. In 1998, at least they won a game before being shown the door by the Indians once more. In the 1999 Division Series, the Sox finally overcame the Indians, only to lose to the Yanks in the ALCS. Boston failed to reach the postseason the next three years, although home attendance exceeded 2.5 million each time.

Then, with new ownership in place, the Sox won no fewer than 93 games in four consecutive years. In 2003, they got by Oakland in the ALDS only to lose a seven-game heartbreaker to New York in the next round. They skunked the Anaheim Angels in the 2004 Division Series. Losing the first three games (including a 19-8 drubbing in Game 3) of the ALCS to the Yankees, Terry Francona's team might well have been making vacation plans. But with steely determination, they proceeded to win Game 4 in 12 innings, Game 5 in 14 innings, and two more in Gotham to shock George Steinbrenner's boys. Johnny Damon, Pedro Martinez, Curt Schilling, Manny Ramirez, Jason Varitek, and the rest made easy work of the National League's St. Louis Cardinals to become World Series champions.

The Curse of the Bambino, if such a thing truly existed, had begun on January 3, 1920 (when Babe Ruth's contract was sold to the Yankees) and ended on October 27, 2004, during a total lunar eclipse (when Edgar Renteria made the Cardinals' 27th out by bouncing back to pitcher Keith Foulke, who very carefully threw the ball to first baseman Doug Mientkiewicz for the final out). Was there really a "curse?" No doubt, some unfortunate things had happened in Sox history over those eight-and-a-half decades, not the least of them being Ruth's development into the most titanic of players. There were valleys, close calls, and maddening episodes galore, but no curse. The phrase itself only gained currency in 1990 when writer Dan Shaughnessy used it as the clever title of a team history. It was nothing more than media-created fluff, carried along by fans so passionate and obsessed with their baseball team that it perplexed those in other parts of the country. At any rate, all such talk ended that night in Busch Stadium.

Q This pitcher, who hailed from Cedar Rapids, Iowa, had already enjoyed a nice career with the Baltimore Orioles, including being MVP of the 1983 ALCS. Then he was traded to the Red Sox and helped them win the AL East in 1988 and 1990. Who was he?

A Mike Boddicker.

Q What AL record did the Boston Red Sox set in 1988?

A They won 24 straight games at home, surpassing the league mark of 22 set by the 1931 Philadelphia Athletics.

Q What was *l'affaire Margo*?

A Boggs, a married man, had a woman on the side named Margo Adams. When this fact became public in 1988, Adams implicated other players for such indiscretions, and the team was thrown into turmoil. Manager John McNamara was fired, and soon Boggs could be seen doing a big mea culpa with Barbara Walters on national TV.

Q And how did Boggs do that season?

A He had one of his best years: a .480 on-base percentage (highest in the majors since Mickey Mantle's .488 in 1962), .366 batting average, 45 doubles, 125 walks, and 128 runs scored.

Q He was a native of nearby Walpole, had managed the Pawtucket minor league team for nine years, and was a scout and coach for the Sox before being hired to manage in 1988 on an interim basis. Who was he?

A Joe Morgan. When the team promptly won its first 12 games, he got the job full-time. His Red Sox finished atop the AL East twice, but he was fired in 1991.

Q This big right-hander had two full seasons (1988 and 1989) with Boston and ended his long career as baseball's all-time saves leader. Identify him.

A Lee Smith. He did save 478 games, but his won-loss record is not so hot (71-92). And in his 18 seasons in the majors, Smith's teams reached the postseason just twice and quickly lost.

Q What is the second-worst trade in the history of the Olde Towne Team?

A Perhaps it was when GM Lou Gorman sent minor leaguer Jeff Bagwell to the Astros in exchange for 37-year-old pitcher Larry Anderson. Over an illustrious 15-year career in Houston, Bagwell hit 449 home runs and was the 1994 National League MVP.

Q What two pitchers share the team record for most career shutouts?

A Cy Young and Roger Clemens, both of whom recorded 38 for Boston. Babe Ruth, short as his pitching career was, had 17.

Q What is the Baseball Beanpot?

A Since 1990, Fenway Park has hosted a regional college baseball tournament, featuring schools like Harvard, Boston College, Boston University, Northeastern, and the University of Massachusetts. It is a spinoff of the Hockey Beanpot, played by the same schools every year since the early 1950s.

Q Who was the last Red Sox player to successfully pull off the hidden-ball trick?

A Second baseman Steve Lyons, who did it against the White Sox in 1991.

Q In 1992, who became the all-time career saves leader (although he was later passed by Lee Smith and Dennis Eckersley)?

A Jeff Reardon. The year after his retirement, he committed armed robbery in a Florida jewelry store but was acquitted because he had been taking anti-depressants and mood stabilizers, and was distraught over his son's recent death.

Q One of only six players to have 300 home runs and 300 stolen bases, he was a designated hitter for the Red Sox in 1993 and 1994. Who was he?

A Andre "the Hawk" Dawson. He had been NL rookie of the year in 1977 with the Expos and MVP in 1987 with the Cubs.

Q This knuckleballer started out with the Pittsburgh Pirates in 1992 before signing with Boston three years later. Despite going from the starting rotation to the bullpen and back, he has become the third-winningest pitcher in franchise history. Who is he?

A Tim Wakefield. He once struck out four batters in an inning—an oddity that can be explained by his fluttering ball getting by the catcher on one of those K's—and gave up six home runs to the Tigers in a game in 2004 but still won.

Q He had been general manager of the Montreal Expos before taking that job with the BoSox in 1994, and he kept it until owner John Henry fired him in 2002. Who is he?

A Dan Duquette. Not an especially popular figure among Fenway fanatics, Duquette is best remembered for saying in 1996 that Roger Clemens was "in the twilight of his career." Of course, Clemens went on to win four more Cy Youngs with other teams. To his credit, however, Duquette brought in such players as Derek Lowe, Pedro Martinez, Johnny Damon, and Jason Varitek.

Q And who brought in Duquette?

A John Harrington. This man had risen from being an accounting professor at Boston College to controller of the American League to treasurer of the Red Sox to CEO. Harrington overhauled the front office, part of which included making Duquette the general manager. The media tended to regard him as a distant and rather mysterious figure.

Q Steroids whistleblower Jose Canseco spent two years (1995 and 1996) with Boston. Did he have anything left by then?

A Yes, although he played strictly as a designated hitter. Canseco hit 52 home runs in those two seasons and had batting averages of .306 and .289. He was soon sent on his merry way, however—back to the A's, then the Blue Jays, Devil Rays, Yankees, Angels, White Sox, Expos, and a couple of embarrassing stints in the minors.

Q This hefty first baseman was American League MVP in 1995 and a major factor in the Red Sox' 1995 and 1998 playoff teams. Name him.

A Mo Vaughn. A popular figure in Boston, he nonetheless battled with the media and the front office, eventually wearing out his welcome. Vaughn, who later played with the Angels and Mets, wore number 42 on his jersey in honor of Jackie Robinson.

Q Who is the only modern-day player to win a World Series ring with both the Yankees and Red Sox?

A Pitcher Ramiro Mendoza (1996, 1998–2000 with New York; 2004 with Boston).

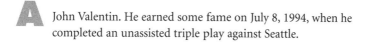

Q This Seton Hall grad spent 10 years with the Red Sox, and was adored by the fans for his solid play at shortstop and his knack for getting big hits in late innings. But when Nomar Garciaparra arrived in 1996, he moved to second base, then to third base, then to the bench, then to the New York Mets. Who was he?

A John Valentin. He earned some fame on July 8, 1994, when he completed an unassisted triple play against Seattle.

Q A teammate of Jason Varitek at Georgia Tech, this man made his presence known with authority as 1997 rookie of the year, hitting 30 homers, driving in 98 runs, and playing like a vet at shortstop. He led the AL in batting in 1999 and 2000, and Red Sox fans absolutely fell in love with him. Who was he?

A Nomar Garciaparra. By 2001, however, he was beginning to struggle with wrist and groin injuries. His performance was not what it had been, and GM Theo Epstein did not feel that Garciaparra's on-base percentage and defense merited the hefty money he was being paid. He was sent to the Cubs and from there went to the Dodgers. He now plays first base, the better to avoid injury.

Q How did Roger Clemens do on July 12, 1997, when he returned to Boston with the Blue Jays?

A He struck out 16 batters and often glared menacingly at the suite of Sox GM Dan Duquette. Clemens won the game and improved to 14-3 on the season.

Q He is a native of the Dominican Republic who played two years with the Dodgers and four with the Expos. It was in Montreal that he developed into one of the best pitchers in baseball. Who is he?

A Pedro Martinez. He came to the Red Sox in November 1997 and signed one of the biggest contracts ever for a pitcher. Records of 23-4 and 18-6 in 1999 and 2000, respectively, proved his value and then some. Fastball, curveball, changeup—all from different angles— he seemed confident of any pitch in any situation. A key figure on the 2003 and 2004 World Series teams, Martinez signed with the New York Mets in 2005.

Q What first baseman batted .500 in the 1999 AL Division Series against Cleveland?

A Mike Stanley.

Q Who, or what, is Wally the Green Monster?

A To the dismay of Boston's traditional fans, this mascot was unveiled during the 1997 season. The kids liked him, but he was the object of many a lusty boo from the start. Nevertheless, Red Sox broadcaster Jerry Remy (an infielder for the team from 1978 to 1984) began discussing Wally's fictitious adventures during slow spots in games, which aided his popularity.

Q A three-time all-American at Georgia Tech, this man took over the Red Sox' catching duties in his rookie season of 1998 and is an unquestioned leader on the team. Who is he?

A Jason Varitek. In July 2004, in a game with the Yankees, he defended one of his pitchers by shoving his glove into the face of Alex Rodriguez, prompting a bench-clearing brawl. The incident sparked the Sox' comeback to win the game and may have been the turning point in the season, as Boston then proceeded to have the best record in the major leagues and, of course, won the World Series.

Q Varitek was named team captain in 2005. Who preceded him in that role?

A It had been vacant since 1989 when Jim Rice retired.

Q What pitcher won 15 games for the Sox in 1998? Hint: For other teams, he threw a no-hitter, won the Cy Young Award twice, and was World Series MVP.

A Bret Saberhagen.

Q Which two BoSox managers have the worst postseason winning percentage?

A Joe Morgan was 0-8, and Kevin Kennedy was 0-3, so both have a meager .000 winning percentage. The best was Bill Carrigan (8-2, .800).

Q And what manager has been in the most postseason games with Boston?

A Terry Francona, with 17 as of 2006. His record is 11-6.

Q What about Francona's baseball background?

A His father, Tito, had a long career with nine big league teams. Terry played college ball at the University of Arizona and then spent a decade as an outfielder/first baseman/DH with the Expos, Cubs, Reds, Indians, and Brewers. Before getting the Sox' gig, he had managed the Phillies for four seasons and coached in Detroit, Texas, and Oakland.

Q What team record does Nomar Garciaparra hold with Fred Lynn, Norm Zauchin, and Rudy York?

A All four drove in 10 runs in a single game.

Q What happened on July 13, 1999, at Fenway Park?

A The All-Star Game was delayed by 15 minutes as Ted Williams rode out in a cart for the first-pitch ceremony. Players from both squads surrounded the former Red Sox star in a show of loving respect.

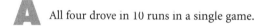

Q What was Troy O'Leary's biggest day with the Red Sox?

A It may have been on October 11, 1999, in Game 5 of the American League Division Series against Cleveland. O'Leary hit two home runs (a three-run shot and a grand slam) to propel his team past the Indians and on to the ALCS against New York.

Q How did it go in Game 3 of the 1999 ALCS?

A Pedro Martinez dominated for seven shutout innings and the Sox roughed up Roger Clemens, giving the New York Yankees their worst loss in postseason history (13-1).

Q What switch-hitting outfielder had 34 homers for the Sox in 2000 and was traded just a year later?

A Center fielder Carl Everett, a loose cannon if ever there was one. The list of his eruptions against opponents, teammates, umpires, and fans is quite long, which is the main reason he played for eight teams over a 13-year career.

Q What happened at Fenway Park on July 15, 2000?

A It was "Family Day," but Everett was ejected from the game for twice bumping home plate umpire Ron Kulpa and then going into a profanity-laced tirade. Everett, who blamed the media, was suspended for 10 games.

Q What are two of the highlights of Trot Nixon's career with the Red Sox?

A On May 28, 2000, at Yankee Stadium, it was a scoreless duel between Pedro Martinez and Roger Clemens (ex–Red Sox star, then with New York). Nixon hit a two-run homer in the top of the ninth to win it. And in the deciding game of the 2004 World Series, his two-out, two-run double off the right field wall of Busch Stadium gave the Sox a 3-0 lead, and that's how it ended.

Q Who pitched a no-hitter for the Red Sox on April 4, 2001?

A Hideo Nomo did it in his Boston debut, beating the Orioles, 3-0. It was the second no-hitter of his career, the first coming in 1996 against Colorado when he was pitching for the Los Angeles Dodgers. Nomo also led the league in strikeouts in '01.

Q This splendid pitcher had won a Cy Young Award, thrown a perfect game, and been on World Series winners before coming to Boston for his finale in 2001. Identify him.

A David Cone.

Q The Red Sox had lost seven straight times to the Yankees in 2001 when their ace pitcher, Pedro Martinez, said what to refute any notions of the Curse?

A "Wake up the Bambino, and I'll drill him in the ass."

Q Name the pitcher who was with Boston in 2001 and 2002 and now sits in a Venezuelan jail on charges of attempted murder.

A Ugueth Urbina.

Q Only recently has Fenway Park been the site for musical concerts. Who has played there?

A Bruce Springsteen & the E Street Band, Jimmy Buffett, the Rolling Stones, Dave Matthews, and Sheryl Crow, among others.

Q What 28-year-old wunderkind became the Sox' GM in 2002?

A Theo Epstein. Raised in nearby Brookline, Massachusetts, he attended Yale and earned a law degree from the University of San Diego. He got his foot in the door as an intern with the Baltimore Orioles and then with the San Diego Padres, but his heart was in Boston. After John W. Henry bought the team in 2002, his president and CEO, Larry Lucchino, named Epstein as the general manager. He was a devoted advocate of sabermetrics, the analysis of baseball through measurement, and objective evidence and methodology. Some people had doubts about his youth and his fancy new way of evaluating players, but they were on board by 2004 when the Sox were World Series champs. Epstein did, however, have one major advantage over all his rivals but one (the Yankees)—a payroll of about $120 million.

Q Lucchino is famous for having coined what term in reference to the New York Yankees?

A He called them "the Evil Empire."

Q Owner John W. Henry certainly has an interesting history. Summarize it.

A His family farmed in Illinois and Arkansas, he attended three colleges in California (but never got a degree), he traveled the country as a professional singer-songwriter, and he was a whiz as a speculator in the commodities markets. Henry made a fortune before purchasing the Florida Marlins (for $158 million) and then, in a complicated deal, swapped them for the Red Sox ($700 million).

Q This native of the Dominican Republic hit 236 homers and drove in 804 runs in eight years (1993–2000) with the Cleveland Indians, and it has been more of the same with Boston. Who is he?

A Manny Ramirez. He led the AL in batting in 2002 (.349) and in home runs in 2004 (43). And, of course, he was MVP of the World Series in the latter season. As an outfielder, Ramirez makes some fine plays and has misadventures, too.

Q How many grand slams does Ramirez have in his career?

A A total of 20, just three behind Lou Gehrig's record.

Q What was the ghoulish aftermath of Ted Williams's death in July 2002?

A At the direction of two of his children (and over the vigorous opposition of a third), Williams's body was flown to an Arizona cryogenics lab. There, his head and body were separated and suspended in liquid nitrogen for reasons that have never been made entirely clear.

Q Who coined the catchphrase "cowboy up" in 2003?

A Outfielder/first baseman Kevin Millar.

Q The phrase "Manny being Manny" refers to Ramirez's mistakes or odd behavior, on and off the field. List three examples.

A On September 9, 2002, in a game against Tampa Bay, he hit a soft grounder and headed straight to the dugout without even moving toward first base. On August 20, 2003, he asked to be pulled from the lineup due to a sore throat but was later seen at a bar with Enrique Wilson of the Yankees. And on July 30 and 31, 2005, he sat out two games in order to "clear his head." Such moments, not to mention his frequent trade requests (in spite of an $18 million contract) have become increasingly maddening to the Red Sox front office and fans.

Q The Sox hit how many home runs in 2003?

A A franchise-record 238.

Q What transpired in the eighth inning of Game 7 of the 2003 ALCS against New York?

A The Sox led, 5-3, and were five outs away from reaching the World Series. Starting pitcher Pedro Martinez had given up three straight hits. Manager Grady Little visited the mound but chose to leave his ace in. Yankees hitter Jorge Posada immediately tied it up. Then, in the 11th inning, Aaron Boone sent Tim Wakefield's knuckleball over the left field fence at Yankee Stadium to win the game and series. Little, for better or worse, was made the scapegoat and was fired in the offseason.

Q Who got three base hits in one inning of a 25-8 defeat of Florida in 2003?

A Johnny Damon. He is one of a handful of major leaguers to ever pull off that feat.

Q Damon played with Kansas City and Oakland before coming to Boston (2002–2005) and then moved down to New York for big money—or *bigger* money. How did he do in his time with the Red Sox?

A It all came together in 2004 when he batted .304, hit 20 home runs, and had 94 RBI. Damon was one of the leaders of the "idiots" as he called them, the loosey-goosey Red Sox who beat the Yankees in the ALCS and the Cardinals in the World Series. He hit two home runs, one of them a grand slam, in Game 7.

Q This young Texan won fame by propelling the Florida Marlins past the New York Yankees in the 2003 World Series. In less than two years, however, he had joined the Red Sox. Who is he?

A Josh Beckett. On May 20, 2006, he became the first Boston pitcher to hit a home run—since the advent of the designated hitter—in an interleague game against the Phillies.

Q When the Red Sox win, fans file out of Fenway to the tune of what song?

A The Standells' "Dirty Water," which includes in its lyrics the phrase, "Oh-oh, Boston, you're my home."

 This right-handed relief pitcher appeared in 11 of Boston's 14 postseason games in 2004, allowing just one earned run over 14 innings. Identify him.

A Keith Foulke.

Q Foulke paid dearly for something he said when he was struggling in the 2005 season. What was it?

A Often booed by the Fenway faithful, he claimed to care nothing about "Johnny from Burger King."

Q In 2004, during the Sox' glorious run to a World Series title, this man combined with Manny Ramirez to become the first pair of American League teammates to hit 40 home runs, drive in 100 runs, and bat .300 since Babe Ruth and Lou Gehrig did it for the Yankees in 1931. Who is he?

A David "Big Papi" Ortiz. In 2005, he finished second in MVP voting (behind Alex Rodriguez of New York) due to one fact—he is almost exclusively a designated hitter. There continues to be a significant debate in baseball circles as to the value of DHs, since they don't play defense. But nobody can deny that Ortiz has a penchant for coming through in big games.

Q Curt Schilling was a proven winner before he came to Boston in November 2003. He had been a major reason the Phillies won the NL pennant in 1993, and his Arizona Diamondbacks won the championship in 2001. What do people most remember about his 2004 postseason performance?

A Schilling had an injured ankle. Pumped full of painkillers and with blood seeping through his sock, he beat the Yankees in Game 6 of the ALCS. And of course, they went on to sweep the Cardinals in the Series.

Q Identify the 28-inch-tall Dominican actor who was adopted as a Red Sox mascot (particularly by Pedro Martinez) during the 2004 postseason.

A That would be Nelson de la Rosa, who died two years later.

Q What was the Doug Mientkiewicz ball controversy?

A Mientkiewicz was a bit player in the 2004 World Series—a pinch runner in one game and a substitute at first base in the other three. He had one at-bat and no hits. The Series ended with the Cards' Edgar Renteria grounding to pitcher Keith Foulke, who tossed the ball underhanded to Mientkiewicz, setting off earth-shaking celebrations, of course. He pocketed the ball and called it his own, irking his employers who wanted it in a museum or at least to share it with Red Sox fans. Although he was technically in the right, Mientkiewicz was faced with an uproar of opposition and finally compromised.

Q Name Boston's top batter in the 2004 World Series.

A Bill Mueller, who had six hits in 14 at-bats for a .429 average.

Q This high-strung pitcher was with the Cardinals during the 2004 World Series (losing Game 1 when Mark Bellhorn hit an eighth-inning homer) and later signed with the Red Sox. Who is he?

A Julian Tavarez. Boston was the eighth major league team for which he would pitch. Tavarez's career with the Sox got off to a bad start when he was suspended 10 games for a spring-training fistfight with a Tampa Bay Devil Rays player.

Q What happened at Fenway on opening day, 2005?

A A banner commemorating the World Series champs was unveiled. It extended the full length and breadth of the Green Monster.

Q Identify the relief pitcher who led the big leagues in appearances in 2005 with 81.

 A Mike Timlin. He had a 7-3 record, 2.24 ERA, and saved 13 games.

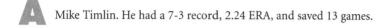

Q What was the longest nine-inning game in major league history?

A It happened quite recently—August 18, 2006. The Yankees and Red Sox were playing the second game of a day–night doubleheader at Fenway Park. Starting at 8:07 p.m. and ending at 12:52 a.m. with a groundout by Boston's Wily Mo Pena, it lasted four hours and 45 minutes. This game, with 10 pitching changes, 437 pitches, and 34 hits, was a 14-11 New York victory.

Q Who broke a 68-year-old franchise record for home runs in 2006?

A David Ortiz, whose 54 exceeded Jimmie Foxx's 50, set back in 1938.

Q This young pitcher played collegiately at Mississippi State, breezed through the minors, and soon took over the closer position from Keith Foulke. Who is he?

A Jonathan Papelbon, whose entrance music at Fenway Park is "Wild Thing" by the Troggs.

Q Name the Japanese pitcher to whom the Red Sox gave a $52 million, six-year contract in December 2006.

A Daisuke Matsuzaka, formerly of the Seibu Lions. MVP of the 2006 World Baseball Classic, he is said to have a 96-mph fastball, a splitter, a changeup, a slider, a curve, and something called a "gyroball."

MORE GREAT SPORT TITLES FROM TRAILS BOOKS

After They Were Packers, *Jerry Poling*

Always a Badger: The Pat Richter Story, *Vince Sweeney*

Baseball in Beertown: America's Pastime in Milwaukee, *Todd Mishler*

Badger Sports Trivia Teasers, *Jerry Minnich*

Before They Were the Packers: Green Bay's Town Team Days,
    Denis J. Gullickson and Carl Hanson

Chicago Bears Trivia Teasers, *Steve Johnson*

Cold Wars: 40+ Years of Packer-Viking Rivalry, *Todd Mishler*

Green Bay Packers Titletown Trivia Teasers, *Don Davenport*

Mean on Sunday: The Autobiography of Ray Nitschke, *Robert W. Wells*

Mudbaths and Bloodbaths: The Inside Story of the Bears-Packers Rivalry,
    Gary D 'Amato and Cliff Christl

New York Yankees Trivia Teasers, *Richard Pennington*

Packers By the Numbers: Jersey Numbers and the Players Who Wore Them,
    John Maxymuk

Vagabond Halfback: The Life and Times of Johnny Blood McNally,
    Denis J. Gullickson

For a free catalog, phone, write, or visit us online.

Trails Books
A Division of Big Earth Publishing
923 Williamson Street, Madison, WI 53703
800.258.5830 · www.trailsbooks.com